VOTING PATTERNS IN A LOCAL ELECTION

by Alvin Boskoff EMORY UNIVERSITY
and Harmon Zeigler UNIVERSITY OF GEORGIA

P9-APW-878

J. B. LIPPINCOTT COMPANY

PHILADELPHIA AND NEW YORK

PREFACE

IN THE MODERN WORLD, there is no need to justify continued interest in, and further understanding of, the *political aspect* of human experience. Political history, political philosophy, and the study of formal governmental structures have made substantial contributions to our knowledge of political institutions. But in recent years, crucial developments in such fields as sociology, social psychology, psychology, political science, and economics have pointed up the need for understanding of political *behavior*. By "political behavior" we mean the actual decisions and activities of individuals (and categories of individuals) in political situations—as well as the motivational and attitudinal variables connected with such behavior. By focusing on political behavior, we believe we can more clearly evaluate the *operation* of political structures and also increase our understanding of the processes by which political systems *change*.

The behavioral focus, which should serve to supplement rather than compete with other approaches, is particularly applicable to the study of *elections* and *voting decisions*. In the present instance, we seek to provide, first, a brief but comprehensive review of behavioral theory and investigation on voting. The major portion of this book, however, describes and analyzes *one case study* of voting patterns in a local election—based on research by the authors. Our primary aim in this research was to locate and assess the importance of (1) status, (2) influence processes, and (3) commitment to the community for the behavior of voters. The information and the issues involved in this work, we hope, will be of interest to the thoughtful citizen—or as he is often called, "the educated layman." But we also believe this material is distinctly appropriate for fruitful use in such college courses as Political Institutions, Interest Groups,

Political Parties, Public Opinion, Local Government, Community Organization, and Social Psychology.

We should point out that this book represents a collaborative effort between a sociologist and a political scientist—an experience we have found to be professionally satisfying and one to be highly recommended. The authors, of course, are jointly responsible for the entire work. However, Boskoff assumed major responsibility for chapters two and three, while Zeigler had similarly special responsibility for chapters one and four. The remaining chapters were truly collaborative projects.

For the benefit of statistical purists, we should likewise point out that we are aware of the shortcomings connected with using chi-square analysis in contingency tables having cells with fewer than five frequencies. In several instances, we have ignored this caution in order to obtain an approximate indication of the probability of independence. The alternative of collapsing categories seemed on some occasions to deprive us of needed distinctions in data. We feel that our discussion is not materially affected by our calculated deviation from convention.

Finally, we gratefully acknowledge assistance and support from the following: Emory University Research Committee, for a grant that made the DeKalb study possible; Emory Computer Center, for data-processing services; our respective students in Sociology and Political Science, who interviewed the sample of county voters; Dr. Jerry L. L. Miller, now of the University of Arizona, who did most of the preliminary statistical analysis; and Dr. John T. Doby, who encouraged the authors in many ways.

ALVIN BOSKOFF

HARMON ZEIGLER

Atlanta and Athens, Georgia
March, 1964

CONTENTS

CONTENTS

CHAPTER 1

THE VOTING DECISION:
BACKGROUND AND THEORY

ELECTIONS AND VOTING constitute an important part of the dramatic ritual of modern society. But we may legitimately focus attention on either or both of two aspects of this crucial type of activity. On one hand, there is the final result of a contest: Who won? By what margin? Which amendment or issue won a majority of the votes? This may be called the practical, empirical emphasis—one that concentrates on political *products*. But an alternative focus is based on the desire to understand how the election results were actually achieved. In short, the emphasis thus shifts to voting as the *culmination* of a series of social processes that affect a definable population of impressionable, stubborn, or apathetic persons. In this way, the final vote may be viewed not as an inevitable outcome, but as one of several possibilities that results from the fortuitous conjunction of numerous

1

similar and divergent pressures and experiences. Consequently, this viewpoint turns from the vote to the *voter*,
thereby seeking to describe and explain the course by which
he and his contemporaries respond to successive appeals for
his allegiance. This may be called the *behavioral approach*
to voting, if it is also understood that "voting behavior" refers to the entire set of acts, attitudes, and opinions that
persons exhibit in some electoral sequence—not just the act
of pulling levers in voting booths.

In a democratic political system, the behavioral approach
to voting is particularly appropriate since the relative free-
dom of choice provides not only a diversity of candidates
and issues but also encourages a variety of attitudes and
numerous opportunities to alter voting intentions and decisions. As a result of this system, furthermore, the traditional
European conception of the electorate as a relatively undif-
ferentiated mass, or as a set of fixed strata, becomes unwork-
able. Instead, the body of eligible voters must be approached
as a complex of broad social segments or categories, with
which voters identify themselves—or transfer allegiances—
over given election periods. In fact, the discovery of these
networks of allegiances and their underlying causes is the
indispensable task of the behavioral approach to voting.

Current trends in evaluating human behavior give increasing emphasis to *decision-making* as a crucial activity in modern society. Much of the fruitful work in economics, psychology, sociology, and political science is concerned with
exploring the complex determinants of decisions by aggre-
gates of persons. For example, we are beginning to probe
into such decisions as choosing a career, moving into a home,
purchasing consumer goods, selecting a mate, and spacing

children. Voting, then, is a whole set of decision-making processes (for individuals, categories, or a whole electorate) in the arena of public issues. Elections confirm and reiterate the need to widen decision-making temporarily but recurrently. They serve to pose issues, crystallize attitudes, generate contradictory feelings, or even to produce boredom and apathy. In any case, from this welter of cues and pressures, voters arrive at intelligible, but not necessarily rational, conclusions that are only partly expressed in the final act of voting or abstaining. Therefore, analyses of voting behavior and underlying social pressures contribute vitally to an understanding of the actual working of our peculiarly viable political system, as well as its subtle interrelations with major institutional patterns of our time.

Voting Research: Retrospect and Prospect

The interest of social scientists in the act of voting is nearly as old as the democratic process, but research reaching beyond speculation and the mere assertion of causal relationships is much more recent. The pioneer study of voting behavior was Stuart Rice's *Quantitative Methods in Politics,* published in 1928.[1]

In this book, Rice explored and elaborated upon the idea that the root of political behavior is the individual attitude. The activity of any individual or group, Rice maintained, could be traced back to a value or perception of the real world. Taking voting as a political action that reflected individual attitudes, Rice investigated the factors that contributed to differing attitudes and hence to difference in direction of votes. While Rice's model of voting choice was individualistic, the variables that he believed contributed to the development of attitudes were social or ecological. He explored the differences in voting patterns between urban and rural areas, shifts in attitudes and votes by the same groups of voters over a period of time, regional distributions of voting preferences, and the relation between a person's attitudes and his perceptions of events and personalities.

A persistent device throughout Rice's book is a somewhat restricted theoretical model of political behavior based upon an attitude scale ranging from "radicalism" to "conservatism." Voters and candidates alike could be placed at any point on the scale, according to the manner in which their attitudes were expressed. Since a person's position on the scale measured his political preference, a basic key to the prediction of electoral outcomes was thought to be the ability of the researcher to ascertain the degree to which a candidate's position approached the dominant attitudes of a particular voting segment.

Such a scheme would seem to present a foolproof device for understanding the voting choice, but such was not Rice's intent. Because of the primitive nature of survey methods in the 1920's, Rice did not inquire into the psychological mechanism of the choice. He merely measured distributions of the final result of the interaction of social and psychological variables. Much of his description of voting behavior of various population groups was based upon aggregate data. Using published election returns and census reports, Rice was able to arrive at some sharp distinctions between voters. These distinctions were arranged along social, occupational, and regional lines. However, such voting distributions could not provide an understanding of the behavior of individual voters. Using a geographical area as the basic unit in the political process might seem to conflict with Rice's theoretical underpinning. While it might be good sense to assume that the way individuals in a voting district behave is directly related to the cumulative choice of the area where they live, the pitfalls of such an assumption are many. As Austin Ranney justifiably concludes, " . . . correlations based upon aggregate data cannot be relied upon to produce reliable descriptions or explanations of the behavior of individuals."[2]

On the other hand, acknowledgment of this shortcoming should not obscure the fact that the behavior of geographical units is *suggestive* of the behavior of individuals and that social scientists can use such data to considerable advantage as long as they do not make inferences about individuals. Students of voting who followed Rice have demonstrated the uses of aggregate data. Perhaps the most noteworthy of such studies is the work of V. O. Key, Jr.[3]

At the time Rice wrote, no one had approached an understanding of the psychology of the individual voter. Voters were regarded as members of certain specified subgroups whose behavior followed, with minimum deviation, the dominant preferences of the group. It was fashionable to speak of an "urban vote" or "rural vote" with the tacit assumption that individual choice was a function of group identification.

SURVEY RESEARCH

These same assumptions carried over into the first survey based on a study of the electoral process. Paul Lazarsfeld, Bernard Berelson, and Hazel Gaudet, in studying the 1940

Presidential election, used the individual voter as a focal point in theory and in research design.[4] The product of this design, *The People's Choice*, not only introduced survey research to the study of voting but also relied upon the "panel" method. Rather than interviewing each person once and allowing him to describe his choice in retrospect, Lazarsfeld, Berelson, and Gaudet approached each member of the selected panel at regular intervals during the campaign and after the election. The panel consisted of 600 residents of Erie County, Ohio, each of whom was interviewed seven times. In this manner the authors presented an explicit theory of individual choice which did not differ greatly from the earlier conclusions of Rice. It was learned that political attitudes are firmly rooted in social interaction. A person's vote was clearly influenced by associates at work, neighborhood groups, primary groups such as the family, socio-economic status, religion, place of residence, and the like.

Thus, even though the data were based upon individual responses, the voting decision was regarded as the end product of the interrelationship of social variables. Political attitudes may well reflect ego-involvement, yet such attitudes are not products of isolation. They develop by means of the individual's identification with objective social groupings. To understand the *why* of voting, one must first ascertain the social background of the voter.

It can be seen quite clearly that *The People's Choice* may be interpreted as a deterministic view of individual choice. The rational, informed voter idealized in traditional democratic theory then becomes a fiction, albeit a pleasing one. The independent voter, instead of being the foundation of true democracy, was described in this view as a somewhat unfortunate individual faced with the problem of conflicting group identifications. Exposed to these cross-currents, he found it difficult to reach a decision and, thus, became apathetic.

The People's Choice showed considerable continuity with *Quantitative Methods in Politics,* the major difference being in the survey method rather than in the empirical findings. Rice had described pervasive political attitudes in terms of special distributions based upon aggregate data; Lazarsfeld, Berelson, and Gaudet treated group consensus with identical respect, but by means of the survey technique they were able to suggest clearer and more exhaustive categories of identification.

Soon after the Erie County study appeared in its second edition, the two senior authors made plans to repeat their panel technique for the study of the 1948 Truman-Dewey campaign and election. The locale chosen for the research was Elmira, New York.[5] A second application of the panel method by the same social scientists who performed the first was bound to be more refined. When the study, *Voting,* appeared in 1954 a new set of possible contributing factors was introduced, but the essential conclusion of the first study— the group basis of voting—was retained with only slight modification. The *pattern* of interaction between the individual and the social group received more attention. Also, the role of issues in the 1948 Presidential campaign and the impact of community structure and values were added to the list of factors influencing the direction of the vote.

Although the number of interviews with each voter was reduced, a much sharper description of the social nature of balloting emerged. With regard to the individual's group identifications, attention was given to the flow of communication (or transmission of information) from the group to the individual and the reactions of the individuals who received the information. As expected, it was found that political discussion takes place almost entirely within politically and socially homogeneous groups. In these circumstances, communication between voters tended to reinforce existing biases rather than to expose the individual to conflicting points of view. Vigorous debate may well take place, but the pressures on the individual to conform to prevailing group sentiments gradually eliminate dissenting opinions. Consequently, as the 1948 campaign neared its climax and became more heated, intragroup solidarity increased while intergroup cleavages and hostilities were magnified and were considered more prominent by the individual.

A vital addition to the group theory of the authors, based upon an omission from the first book, is a description of the role of community organization, structure, and values in the electoral process. This added material is doubly important because, although the data concern national elections, the implications for local voting behavior are not to be ignored. The authors regard formal organizations, such as labor unions or business groups, as institutionalized cleavages between groups within the community. In this role such organizations perform the important task of political socialization—the learning of political values. Political socialization is aimed only at members of the organizations, and not at the general public. To illustrate, labor unions did not appear to be very effective in reaching an appreciable segment of the population of Elmira, but they did establish communication with their own membership.

Having decided that formal organizations are most effective with their own membership, the authors present detailed evidence of interaction between the individual and the organization. All members do not react in the same manner to the dissemination of information by an organization. Rather, the degree to which an individual identifies with the group is a crucial variable in determining the degree to which he will conform to its ideology. Thus, the more a person participates in the affairs of his organization, the more probable it is that he will agree with its official position. While most members of labor unions were Democratic in their voting preference, such preference increased in direct relation to the extent of their participation in union affairs. By discussing organization-individual interaction, *Voting* presents the individual with somewhat more "non-group" choice than was attributed to him in *The People's Choice.*

A final aspect of *Voting* deserves mention because of its usefulness in studying local voting behavior. This aspect is what the authors term community "atmosphere." Admittedly, the atmosphere of a community is a much more transitory factor than group identification, which is more easily measurable. However, the firmly Republican atmosphere of Elmira was found to be sufficiently institutionalized in the structure of the community to have objective manifestations. The effect of community atmosphere is, of course, rooted in the distribution of values among the social classes of the community, and it is not considered to be some phenomenon that exists beyond the social values of the community's residents. However, the atmosphere does not involve all voters equally. In the event that the social affiliations of a voter conflict—that is, the individual has become subject to cross-pressures—the Republican atmosphere *might* become an important variable.

Obvious difficulties in locating and describing the agencies by which community atmosphere is transmuted into operational definitions by individuals prevented full development of the concept. Yet ideas of the "character" of a community have been treated in more detail by students of local institutions and politics with results generally in accordance with the suggestions of *Voting*. A homogeneous community consensus is, of course, an ideal type. However, at the risk of dangerous generalization, one could say that the character of a community, to the extent that such character is given political expression, becomes more discernible as the size of the community decreases. Elmira, a small city in upstate New York, would thus exhibit more homogeneity in values than a larger city with more varied social groupings. For example, community atmosphere or character is a typical device used to describe the politics of *suburban* communities. Thus Scott Greer writes that "the disappearance of the party label . . . means that elected officials are largely middle class Republicans. The basic dominance of business ideology, the businessman as first-class citizen, is sharply evident in suburbia."[6]

THE SURVEY RESEARCH CENTER

Voting marked the end of an era in the study of Presidential elections by means of survey research. The entrance of the Survey Research Center of the University of Michigan into the field of surveys of political attitudes marked the beginning of an orientation away from social variables as basic causal factors, and toward the consideration of *psychological attributes* as crucial variables. The orientation of the Survey Research Center was, from the beginning, in the direction of social psychology rather than sociology; psychological attitudes were regarded as more reliable predictors of direction of vote than conformity to group standards.

The idea of reciprocity in the interactions between individuals and their environment, which was suggested to some extent in *Voting*, was raised to a position of primary importance in the Survey Research Center's analysis of the 1952 Eisenhower-Stevenson campaign, *The Voter Decides*.[7] The study, with its emphasis on psychological variables, was a significant break with the past, but it is also of extreme importance that the study was based on a *national* probability sample rather than a local one, thus eliminating the possibility of the influence of community structure upon the vote.

The Voter Decides, in fact, virtually ignores background factors, such as socio-economic status or religious affiliation, in favor of a careful analysis of the interaction among three "intervening" attitude variables: party identification, issue orientation, and candidate orientation. It is clear that the authors, Angus Campbell, Gerald Gurin, and Warren E. Miller, regard these attitudes as existing somewhat independently of social variables because very little attention is given to determining how these attitudes develop. The authors are not saying that the ecological variables that were hitherto regarded as sufficient did not exist or were not important. What they do suggest is that the *intervening* psychological variables are more reliable as tools for prediction.

The conscious neglect of ecological variables—even to the extent of not considering how psychological variables are

established and maintained—suggests a description of the
individual voter responding to internal psychological drives
rather than to group-imposed norms. Concerning the Survey
Research Center's treatment of psychological and social
variables, Peter Rossi writes: "For the authors, socio-economic status could only operate on the voter's candidate
preferences through the effect it might have on such motivational variables as party identification. Hence the relationship which socio-economic status might have to voting is
regarded as a false correlation which would disappear once
the proper motivational variables were held constant." [8]

There is no doubt that *The Voter Decides* presented a dramatic reversal of trends in survey analysis. On the other
hand, it should be reiterated that the move toward psychological variables was one of strategy. The authors engaged
in a conscious choice of factoring out psychological variables
and building a monograph around them. As the Survey Research Center continued its research, it expanded its theoretical model and, while not modifying its initial concern
with psychological causes of voting behavior, placed these
variables within the context of a broader political system.
Enjoying the advantage of a permanent organization and
thus using the opportunity of establishing continuities by
building upon the past, the Survey Research Center has
been able to record and interpret trends in electoral behavior over a period of time. In so doing, the Center has
moved social variables away from their former deterministic
nature—a trend that V. O. Key feared might "take the politics out of the study of electoral behavior"—and placed them
within the framework of a wider matrix of contributory factors.[9]

It can not be maintained that ecological characteristics have no place in electoral analysis any more than it is empirically justifiable to attribute sole causal force to them. What is needed is an understanding of the conditions under which voting decisions approach the deterministic model of the pioneer works as well as of the conditions under which individual decisions are less dependent upon perceptions of class interests. What the work of the Survey Research Center suggests is that the strength of the relationship between status and vote is subject to considerable short-term variations. To give this variation more meaning, the idea of "status polarization" is introduced.[10] This idea rests upon an understanding of social class as a *psychological reality,* which is dependent upon the degree to which an individual structures his behavior in terms of his perceptions of his class membership. Such perceptions are changeable; they do not persist without mutation. Hence, polarization is that condition in which status groups have expressed antagonism, and members of social classes are aware of such hostility.

In *The American Voter,* Angus Campbell, Philip Converse, Donald Stokes, and Warren Miller, all of the Survey Research Center, discuss polarization on the basis of a hypothetical continuum ranging from depolarization to complete polarization.[11] Although they do not maintain that society ever mirrors one of these ideal types, they do argue that, at certain periods of history, it is possible to see an approximation between the real world and the ideal type. In a condition of complete depolarization, knowledge of a person's status would be of no value in predicting an individual's vote; in a condition of complete polarization, on the other hand, such knowledge would be of great value. Thus, while we know that lower status groups "normally" favor the Democratic Party and higher status groups favor the Republican Party, this does not make it possible to predict future voting behavior, since the role of social class is dynamic rather than static.

In an article appearing prior to the publication of *The American Voter*, Philip Converse gives a concise account of variations in polarization. He points to a net decline in status polarization with the notable exception of the 1948 election and relates these fluctuations to the salience of perceptions of external threats to national survival. Hence:

The temporary evaporation of the most burdensome foreign problems, along with the sudden unleashing of pent-up class-relevant actions, particularly the great post-war strikes in major industries, the struggle in Congress to place legislative controls on the activities of labor unions, and the development of first anxieties concerning an "inevitable" post-war depression, all must have contributed to a rise in the relative salience of domestic economic issues which had remained dormant during the war.[12]

Not only are social variables subject to change in importance according to the nature of external events, but it is also likely that perceptions of salience vary from class to class. Also, one could hardly overlook the possibility that the manner in which a campaign is conducted can contribute to or detract from polarization. In *The American Voter*, the authors use an intriguing metaphor, the funnel of causality, in order to give social variables a more stable position within a general causal theory of the voting decision. If the mouth of the funnel represents the act of voting, we can assign social variables a place further away from the mouth and psychological variables closer to it: "It follows from the fact of remoteness that these [social] concepts tend to account for much less variance than do attitudinal materials drawn closer to the behavior." [13]

LOCAL VOTING BEHAVIOR: THE BASIC CHARACTERISTICS

We have treated the development of survey research on Presidential elections primarily to call attention to the decline of status as a sole predictive device. Turning now to an examination of local voting behavior, we find no comparable development. Whether it is due to the failure of funding organizations to subsidize surveys of comparable sensitivity to those of the Survey Research Center on local elections, the fact remains that the local voting decision is explored more in the theoretical tradition of *Voting* than of *The American Voter*. It is possible, of course, that the local voting pattern is more anchored to social variables. At any rate, psychological "intervening" variables have not been used to describe the mechanics of the local vote. In lieu of any clear evidence on this matter, it is possible to extract some theoretical clues from studies of national elections to suggest a possible explanation for the persistence of class in local voting.

It was mentioned earlier that class awareness may differ from stratum to stratum. In *The American Voter* it was suggested that status identification is most likely to occur among sophisticated, politically active individuals. Hence, in Presidential elections, status polarization is not necessarily related to turnout. One might assume the opposite to be true, but the 1948 election—described by Converse as a highly polarized election—generated a low turnout. If we find high status polarization in national elections with low turnout, we should certainly expect to find it at the local level. It would not require a very penetrating analysis of local voting behavior to come to the conclusion that local elections do not attract voters to the same degree that state or national elections do. Some of the earliest studies of local elections made much of the relatively apathetic local electorate. Especially noteworthy are the writings of Charles H. Titus, Roscoe C. Martin, Harold F. Gosnell, and James K. Pollock.[14] Out of the writings of these social scientists emerged a series of generalizations that have been refined by contemporary writers: (1) local elections are characterized by low turnout; (2) local elections for public office attract more voters than do elections for bond issues, charter amendments, and various "non-personal" referenda; and (3) in either type of election there is usually greater participation among high status groups than among the more impoverished strata.

Since local elections attract a disproportionate share of voters from the upper classes, it follows that a high-turnout local election will gain the added voters from the lower strata and that it will take an unusually heated election to do so. However, when such an election does occur it is usually typified by exaggerated appeals to class interests. Under normal circumstances the local electorate can be understood as consisting of two categories of voters: those who are persistently informed and interested and establish their interest by attending the various civic meetings, reading about local affairs, and voting in the low-turnout type of elections; and those who care very little about local affairs and vote only occasionally. These occasional votes can produce real trouble for local officials. In the typical local election, the interested, high-status citizens comprise the active electorate. If the election attracts an unusually large number of voters, the increase will be taken from groups of people whose interest in the community is minimal. In the case of non-personal elections—those for bond issues and the like—there is a fairly well established relation between the size of the vote and the probability of a favorable vote, that is to say a vote in favor of the bond issue, fluoridation of water, or home rule charter. The higher the turnout, the less the probability of a favorable vote.[15] On this subject R. D. McKenzie wrote some years ago that "so-called moral and patriotic questions, especially when the issues are definitely associated with human personalities, invariably call forth a much higher vote than do questions of municipal policy with much greater intrinsic importance, such as the installation of a municipal water system, the introduction of a new city charter, or the purchase of a street railway."[16] As long as the vote on such issues remains low, it can be taken to indicate that the normally uninvolved citizens have not reacted to a local proposal except in terms of disinterest. The high-turnout elections—meaning the more controversial ones—have, of course, attracted more attention, and voting has generally been described as in conformity with class positions.

Documentation of the prevalence of low turnout can be pursued almost *ad nauseam*. Gosnell observed that 85 of 114 bond issues considered by the citizens of Chicago between 1924 and 1935 attracted less than one-half of the registered voters, even though there was substantial interest in the outcome of the elections on the part of real estate boards and other local organizations who feared the possibility of a tax increase if the issues were approved.[17] These comments about group involvement are included because of the generally supported hypothesis that participation increases with the amount of controversy the issues in a local election are able to generate. Yet the consistent participation by interest groups did not bring turnout in bond issue elections up to a level approaching the turnout in state, national, or even local elections involving personalities.

Recent studies have reached conclusions not unlike those of Gosnell. While mayoralty elections in New Orleans can attract between 70 and 85 per cent of the registered voters, elections to the less prominent and less controversial (in 1955) school board attracted from 26 to 33 per cent.[18] Even when the election is conducted in a highly emotional atmosphere—for example, the introduction of racial issues in southern elections—the turnout is still low.

Two studies of elections in southern cities, each involving the highly charged issue of race, illustrate the persistent low interest in local elections of the potential electorate. In Memphis, the entry of a Negro candidate into the contest for public works commissioner presented the voters with a personified challenge to their *status quo*. Although the election produced the greatest turnout in the history of the city (129,870 as compared with a previous high of 86,870), this still represented about a 58 per cent turnout.[19] In Little Rock, in the aftermath of the integration of Central High School, segregationists were successful in arranging for an election to determine whether members of the school board (principally those who were suspected of not resisting integration with the expected vigor) should be retained or dismissed. Intensive campaigning by CROSS (Committee to Retain Our Segregated Schools) and STOP (Stop This Outrageous Purge) and all the emotionalism attendant upon elections with exaggerated racial themes generated a 57 per cent response.[20]

Such elections are, of course, unusual and the turnout is higher than normal for local elections. Under more settled conditions, elections involving issues or candidates without any necessary appeal to ego-involved attitudes, the turnout can be expected to be substantially lower. Thus Lawrence O'Rourke refers to a "small core of citizens" which sustains municipal government in Los Angeles County.[21] This hard core will usually be drawn from the relatively high status groups within the community, those who feel that they have a stake in the outcome of community elections. In addition to socio-economic status, length of residence appears to be related to participation in local elections. Those who have lived in the community longest are most likely to take an interest in what may appear to be trivial decisions. Most of these factors contributing to sustained participation can be summed up under the heading of "civic responsibility" or "community identification."

An interesting exception to this generalization has been discovered by students of suburban politics, particularly Scott Greer. He argues that the suburbs, where high status groups are concentrated, do not achieve any higher turnout in local elections than does the central city, which contains more of the lower status groups.[22] It has been suggested that controversy increases participation; but there usually is not very much happening in the suburbs to create a genuinely controversial election. Elections are typically less emotion-

ally charged than those in central cities, perhaps because the
suburbs are more homogeneous in social structure. Hence,
issues in suburban campaigns usually approach the insignificant. Greer indicates the limited appeal of suburban political issues and makes much of the fact that they center
around a few matters of considerably less impact than those
in national elections. He suggests that the suburban political system is consequently ignored by a large portion of its
residents.[23] Hence, high status groups in suburban communities do not play the usually ascribed role. Such a conclusion
was suggested by a study of an election to determine
whether or not to establish a metropolitan government for
the greater St. Louis area. While turnout in the areas outside
the city limits was 40 per cent as compared to 20 per cent
within the city, there was a positive correlation between low
participation and high socio-economic status in the county.
Of course, this election was not of the trivial sort that is
presumed to be typical of those involving only suburban
areas, but it does suggest the apathy of the suburban voter,
irrespective of his socio-economic status. In the city, the correlation between participation and status was "as expected."
High rate of participation and high socio-economic status
were positively correlated.[24]

Excluding the suburban pattern of participation, we can
summarize by describing local elections as falling into one
of two categories: those having little controversy, which attract only the most dedicated local activists; and those that
excite the normally passive portions of the population to
temporary activity. In neither case can we expect a depolar-
ized status situation to be characteristic of the election. In
the low interest election, the dominant participants are the

sophisticated few described in *The American Voter* as being more conscious of their class. In the highly charged election, the temporary participants are stimulated to activity on the basis of class-anchored values—for instance the fear of racial integration on the part of low status whites in southern cities.

THE INFLUENCE OF SOCIAL VARIABLES

Turning now to the question of *how* people vote, rather than who votes, we find that research continues to stress social variables. One question that recurs throughout the literature is the predictive capacity of social variables in an electoral system characterized by its nonpartisan structure. An important aspect of the national election system is the degree to which both major parties convey an "image" to voters. Since in many local elections party labels are absent, the problem is to ascertain the extent to which "national" Democrats or Republicans vote in local elections in a manner consistent with their national inclinations, even without the image of the party as a guide. Are there correlations between national and local voting patterns?

In recent national elections there is not much doubt about the fact that the suburbs support Republican candidates while the central city supports Democrats, a far from startling conclusion due to the preponderence of high socioeconomic status groups in the suburbs.[25] However, the existence of persistent patterns in national politics is not sufficient reason to presume that the patterns are repeated at the local level. Indeed, V. O. Key's study of *partisan* elections in Ohio counties suggests quite strongly that there is an independent quality about local elections.[26] Key found that, while there is a clear tendency for local politics to reflect national trends, there are conspicuous exceptions to this rule. In years of great Republican Presidential strength there is a hard core of Democratic counties that successfully resist the trend; the same is true of certain Republican counties in years of Democratic upsurge at the national level. Resistance is highest when the gap between the voting strength of the parties is diminished. As the gap widens, the correlation between national and local voting patterns increases. This suggests that local political power groupings can perpetuate themselves in defiance of national trends.

If local partisan elections are to some extent independent of national elections, we could hardly expect less of local *nonpartisan* elections. There is no simple conclusion to be reached, however. In a study of nonpartisan elections in California, Eugene C. Lee found that, during a period in which the Democratic Party was increasing its percentage of state and national legislative seats from 39 to 60 per cent, its percentage of local offices increased by only 5 per cent.[27] Of course this does not, except indirectly, provide any information about the relation between different sets of votes. Lee's findings would suggest the same sort of local resistance that Key discovered. Yet when simple correlations between local and national election results are computed, it is quite common to find a strong correlation. That is to say, the same social groups that support the Democratic or Republican parties nationally are able to identify and support local candidates who espouse programs consistent with the national partisan values of the groups.

In an early study of Seattle, Calvin Schmid found that

local nonpartisan voting patterns were highly correlated with national partisan ones.[28] For instance, the vote for the Republican gubernatorial candidate and the vote for a mayoralty candidate with a "Republican" point of view was .95. More recent research of the same nature reaches similar conclusions. Williams and Adrian found a high correlation between votes for local "prevailing slates" and votes for Republican gubernatorial candidates, but are emphatic in insisting that this correlation does not imply that local voters perceive the local slates of candidates as appendages to national parties.[29] In fact, a high correlation does not mean that voters were necessarily aware of the party affiliations of local candidates. While there are some nonpartisan elections in which party organizations play a major role, there are more in which partisan organizations do not function.[30] This is especially true in suburbs and small towns in which a "politics of acquaintance" replaces partisan politics. Consequently, in large cities with a more heterogeneous population and more elections oriented to issues, voter identification of local candidates with partisan values can be expected to be fairly high.

One might conclude that the relation between local and national voting depends to some extent upon the degree to which the structure of the community enables local Democratic and Republican social groupings to identify local issues with party images. This idea is implied by two studies of local politics in very different circumstances: Edward Banfield's description of Chicago and J. Leiper Freeman's analysis of voting in "Bay City" (a Massachusetts industrial city of 50,000).[31]

Chicago might well be considered a good example of Scott

Greer's nation of the "schizoid polity." [32] Banfield describes voting in Chicago in terms of the migration of social classes. In the slums and semi-slums of the city, where the ethnic variable is most conspicuous, the local minority groups populate the Democratic heartland. As one moves out of the city the Democratic vote declines and social status increases. Some of the outlying wards within the city are Republican and the "country towns" (suburbs) are almost entirely so. As the white middle classes move to the suburbs, their places are taken by Negroes and poor southern migrants; hence the Democratic portion of the vote in the inner city is increasing. The social structure of Chicago has been institutionalized by geographical isolation. Differences between the areas of Chicago and the suburbs are obvious and the patterns of voting are equally conspicuous: "the central city-suburban cleavage is the fundamental fact of party politics in the metropolitan area." [33] This basic element is rooted not just in party identification but in pervasive differences in outlook, which in turn are linked to status.

In Bay City, an equally sharp division of the population exists. Freeman explains that the Democrats have "won the battle of demography." [34] The local elections are held under a nonpartisan system, but Democratic social groups (Roman Catholic, non-Yankee, blue collar, less educated) support the local "Progressives," while the Republican groups (Protestant, Yankee, white collar, better educated) vote for the local "Non-partisans." The dominant social and cultural cleavages have adopted a legally nonpartisan system to a partisan reality.

In both these studies the basic unit for analysis is the group; local politics is described as a struggle between social classes, and the individual voter is included in the analysis only as a member of a class. Add the ingredient of place of residence, and the picture of local voting behavior is complete. When low status groups are presented with a candidate or issue capable of identification with the national Democratic image, local and national voting patterns tend to become indistinct.

CLASS AND COMMUNITY STRUCTURE

On the other hand, it is impossible not to consider local situations in which the issues are sufficiently unique as to produce substantial differences between local and national voting patterns. In some cases local elections generate coalitions of groups, which break up in national elections and remain separate until the next local election. For example, James Curley of Boston, while capturing two-thirds of the Irish and Italian vote, still managed to pick up about one-third of the Yankee-Republican vote.[35] A more equal fusion can be found in some southern cities undergoing the strain of transition from the racial *status quo*. In Atlanta and Little Rock, upper income whites and lower income Negroes vote together in favor of moderate candidates against the segregationist candidates supported by lower income whites.

One of the best examples of the blurring of class lines can be found in Robert Dahl's study of New Haven.[36] In the old days, local politicians played the game of "ethnic politics" with regularity: the Irish were in one party and the Yankees in another (much as in Bay City). However, the Republicans successfully worked out a base of support among the

Italians. The Democrats sought to employ the same tactics but lost too many votes in other sections of town when they ran Italian candidates. Such ethnic politics does not exist to any appreciable extent today in New Haven. In fact, there has been a decline in the correlation between the Democratic percentage of the vote and the percentage of foreign born per ward. Dahl argues that ethnic politics, at least in New Haven, is no more than a transitional phase. As assimilation progresses, new loyalties take the place of the old ethnic identifications. By the 1950's, local candidates drew support that cut across ethnic lines. To illustrate, the vote in mayoralty elections in New Haven's 13th Ward (high income, high education, low proportion of foreign-born) has become quite similar to that of the 14th Ward, which is heavily populated by people of Irish descent.

What Dahl seems to suggest is that the issues of local politics are not such as to create status polarization. By studying the trend of local political behavior through time, Dahl thus reaches conclusions that enable one to speculate that the social variable orientation toward local voting may need some modification. However, studies of other communities do not reach similar conclusions. In many communities, the issues of urban politics seem to produce consistent status polarization. This is especially true of elections involving the resolution of issues affecting the course of the community, without regard to the election of local officials. When the issue is one of a bond program, a charter amendment, or the creation of a metropolitan form of government, the citizens do not view the problem in a unified way, but rather as members of social groupings with varying stakes in the community. For example, although in some instances the ownership of property has been correlated with opposition to bond issues and metropolitan governments (perhaps because of the fear of tax increases), there is a reasonable consistency between high socio-economic status and support for various local "reforms." [37]

In one sense, groups whose national political affiliation is predominantly Republican have responded to the demands of changes in local conditions with more vigor than the less affluent groups. Plaut's study of a local water fluoridation election suggests that there is a strong correlation between support for fluoridation and Republican identification. Community leadership was drawn from the business community —the well-educated upper middle classes. Opposition to this leadership and hence to fluoridation was concentrated in the low income Democratic areas.[38]

Socio-economic status, however, cannot function as the lone predictor of voting, since place of residence is of some importance. The studies of the St. Louis election on metropolitan reform indicate that, while there was a positive correlation between socio-economic status and vote for charter revision, the plan was more consistently opposed in St. Louis County than in the city.[39] On the other hand, studies in Cleveland indicate little difference between suburbs and central city areas in support of metropolitan reform. While the tendency is for the suburbs to be more favorably inclined, in contrast with St. Louis, there is no clear "suburban vs. central city" voting pattern. Yet even here, place of residence apparently affects the role of status variables. There is, for example, a positive correlation between socio-economic status and support for metropolitan reform in the areas *outside* the central city. In the city, on the other hand, the less wealthy classes (with the notable exception of Negro voters, who fear a loss of power to the suburbs) provide the greatest proportionate strength in favor of reform.[40]

In summary, while local politics has been described by means of social variables as predictors, the deviations that occur in the instances discussed above suggest that the use of psychological variables would be of great value. On the other hand, the suggestion that local politics is not marked by an automatic translation of social variables into political behavior should not be taken to mean that class is of little consequence. Indeed, it appears likely that the voter in local elections reflects more "class awareness" than the national voter.

In any case, the continued analysis of local elections as a behavioral phenomenon, with particular emphasis on the factors that explain individual and group voting decisions, seems to offer great promise for needed refinements in theories of political behavior. The research that forms the basis for this work was specifically directed toward the problems discussed in this chapter, but it was clearly recognized from the outset that the contributions of this study would necessarily be more suggestive than definitive in nature. However, we believe several significant aspects should be briefly presented at this point.

First, our study was made in a dynamic portion of the Atlanta metropolitan area: DeKalb County. As the most important urbanized area in the Southeast, Atlanta is a particularly rich source of data on the social and cultural adjustments of a relatively new metropolis that is increasingly acquiring "non-Southern" characteristics.

Second, the research and analysis in succeeding chapters

reflect a rewarding interdisciplinary venture in which a sociologist and a political scientist were enabled to pursue an important problem that is nevertheless at the borders of their respective fields.

Finally, the general character of our findings and the discovery of "deviant" or unanticipated patterns have compelled us to re-examine and re-evaluate prevailing theoretical trends in both political science and sociology. Consequently, at several points in chapters 3 through 6, we have set forth a number of empirically oriented speculations about political behavior, which we hope will encourage more creative and more successful investigations.

CHAPTER 2

DEKALB COUNTY:
THE SOCIO-ECONOMIC SETTING
OF THE BOND ELECTION

OF THE FIVE counties in the Atlanta Standard Metropolitan Area, DeKalb County is probably the most varied and dynamic—except for Atlanta's own Fulton County. Yet at the turn of the century, DeKalb was predominantly rural, with a population less than one-tenth of its present size. Indeed, in 1822, DeKalb included all of the present Fulton County; not until 1845 was the small community of Marthasville renamed Atlanta, after which (in 1853) Fulton County became a separate entity. Around this time, the city of Decatur (the county seat of DeKalb) was the only sizable population center, and gave promise of development without much competition from its neighbors.[1]

After 1900 DeKalb and its future were increasingly tied to the adjacent regional metropolis of Atlanta. Since then,

DeKalb has profited by Atlanta's increasing stature as an industrial, transportation, commercial, and financial capital of the Southeast. Much of this has occurred since 1950, however, as a slightly delayed reaction to the economic opportunities following the end of World War II.

DeKalb's rapid development may be indicated in two ways. First, population size has increased dramatically since 1940, following substantial increases during the period 1900-1940. Since 1950 the population has more than doubled, but even more important is the fact that currently over 70 per cent of the population resides in urban concentrations. (By "urban" is meant a community of 2,500 or more, or an area with a minimum density of 500 dwelling units per square mile.) However, the eight incorporated municipalities of the county together account for only about 33,000 persons.[2] Most of the county's "urban" population is actually suburban in character.

TABLE 1

DeKalb County Population, 1900-1963

1900	21,112
1910	27,881
1920	44,051
1930	70,278
1940	86,942
1950	136,395
1960	256,786
1963	285,000 (est.)

A second significant aspect of growth is economic. While many residents commute to jobs in Atlanta and other areas of Fulton County, DeKalb is no longer simply a dormitory county. Since the early 1950's industrial development has

been persistently encouraged, while the previously described
population expansion has been accompanied by a corresponding increase in public service jobs. As a consequence,

TABLE 2

POPULATION GROWTH OF INCORPORATED COMMUNITIES
IN DEKALB COUNTY, 1940 TO 1960

Area and Voting Precinct	1940 No. of Persons	1950 No. of Persons	Per Cent Growth 1940-50	1960 No. of Persons	Per Cent Growth 1950-60
Atlanta in DeKalb (prec. 31-34)	28,994	37,535	22.6	41,332	10.1
Decatur (23, 24, 28, 29)	16,561	21,635	23.5	22,026	1.8
Chamblee (3)	1,081	3,445	68.6	6,635	92.6
Clarkston (13)	921	1,165	20.9	1,524	30.8
Doraville (4)	300	472	36.4	4,437	840.0
Avondale Estates (25)	569	1,070	46.8	1,646	53.8
Lithonia (46)	1,554	1,538	− 1.0	1,667	8.4
Pine Lake (40)	88	566	84.4	738	30.4
Stone Mountain (14)	1,408	1,899	25.8	1,976	4.1
North Atlanta (2)	1,365	5,930	77.2	12,661	113.5
Total Incorporated Population	52,841	75,265	42.4	94,642	25.7
Total Unincorporated Population	34,101	61,130	79.3	162,140	165.2

Source: Department of Planning, *Population Report, DeKalb County,
Georgia,* May, 1963, p. 23.

it is estimated that 75,000 residents leave the county daily
to work; 38,000 residents work within the county; and about
10,000 come to DeKalb jobs from neighboring counties.

The *variety* of occupational opportunities is as important as the constantly increasing supply. The largest source of jobs is the Buick-Oldsmobile-Pontiac assembly plant, which employs more than 6,000. Second in employment is Emory University and its related hospital and clinic services (about 4,300 employees) followed by the county school system (2,900 employees), county administrative services (1,900 workers), and a regional office of the Internal Revenue Service (1,500 workers). In addition, there are dozens of industrial and processing plants: notably Kraft Foods, the Union Bag Company, Frito-Lay (potato chips), General Electric, and the Scottdale Mills (textiles). In the last three years, the federal government established a growing research center, the U. S. Communicable Diseases Center, with over 600 employees, within walking distance of Emory University Hospital. Finally, the county is served by four large suburban shopping centers—each a complex of fifteen or more varied retail outlets.

In fact, the economic (and particularly the industrial) aspect of DeKalb County has reached such proportions that in 1962, for the first time, industrial growth gains exceeded residential growth gains. In short, a more balanced tax burden for home owners and business enterprises is coming to characterize this metropolitan county, replacing the image of the overtaxed suburban county.

As a result of its location and the economic ascendancy of Atlanta, DeKalb reflects a complex process of transition, which is most visible in the development of fluid divisions or zones. Starting at its western boundaries, we may note the extension of Atlanta's municipal limits in the form of a large, irregular finger in southwest DeKalb. This area is predominantly lower class and lower middle class in income and housing. In addition, residents of this area find themselves in double jeopardy: they pay taxes both to Atlanta and to De-Kalb County. (See map on page 124.)

North of this urban pseudopod is a constantly enlarging suburban arc, which is served by five major east-west arteries (and their numerous asphalt tributaries). Virtually all of this area is unincorporated; in general, the older segments are closer to Atlanta, while newer subdivisions have been carved out of the rural fringe near major highways. The symbolic center of this zone is Emory University, its adjacent hospitals, and the U. S. Communicable Diseases Center. In the last six years, the dominant residential pattern of one-family homes has been supplemented by a series of apartment houses (some with swimming pools) that cater to young transient families with substantial incomes.

At either end of the suburban arc is a limited number of small, incorporated "urban" centers. In the north are the industrial suburbs of North Atlanta, Chamblee, and Doraville, while south of the arc is Decatur, the county seat and a locale for small business and small professional enterprises.

Finally, the entire eastern third of the county is rural or rural fringe in character, with somewhat lesser sympathy and understanding of the urbanizing influence of Atlanta than is found among residents in other zones of the county.

In the last decade, the suburban and urban zones have become more representative of the county's population. More important, these areas demand continually expanding public services from the county. In 1957, the first good-sized bond issue ($12,000,000) was approved for such purposes, but by a thin majority. However, in view of the increasing migration into DeKalb—largely in the suburban arc —schools, roads, parks, sanitary facilities and the like, quickly became inadequate. It is estimated that a net of 15,000 citizens are added each year, by migration or birth. Consequently, by 1961, the fruits of the 1957 bond issue were exhausted. After considerable discussion, the county commissioners concluded that a new bond issue, totaling $22.9 million was required as a practical "investment" in the future, despite the recency of the previous bond issue.

In May 1961, county officials initiated a series of public meetings to determine which county needs merited priority in the new bond issue. The results of about sixty exploratory meetings convinced county leaders that the following ten items constituted a necessary package: [3]

1. A modern incinerator plant	*cost* $2,400,000
2. An expanded health center	450,000
3. Branch libraries in four areas, plus expansion of the central library	550,000
4. Five new fire stations	200,000
5. Extension and improvement of the sewer system	3,500,000
6. Water mains for five areas	1,250,000
7. Road and highway improvements	8,410,000
8. Administration building (offices, courts, education department)	3,000,000
9. Parks (new accessions and improvements in existing parks)	2,600,000
10. County airport improvements	540,000
Total	$22,900,000

During late spring and in the intervening period before the October 10 election, county officials traveled throughout the county, explaining the proposed bond program to scores of local groups. The campaign was organized around three themes. First, the nature of each capital improvement was to represent the wishes of the residents of each affected area. For example, a proposed park in a given area could include expenditures for tennis courts, a community center, or a swimming pool, depending on the amount of allocated funds and the expressed needs of probable users. Second, the bond issue was necessary for the continued growth and progress and desirability of DeKalb as a community. Finally —and this was a source of much discussion, misunderstanding, and incredulity—it was repeatedly asserted that the bond issue would not require an increase in the prevailing tax rates. Instead, it was anticipated that increased tax revenue from new businesses and the greater number of home owners would be adequate to finance the cost of borrowing $22.9 million. Indeed, the county tax digest had averaged an increase of $42 million in the preceding four years, while the 1960 increase alone had climbed to $51 million.

These themes received extensive support from various organizations, including the county Chamber of Commerce, the League of Women Voters, both Atlanta newspapers, and the county weekly newspapers. The DeKalb Research-Information Bureau, a recently organized unit, provided a continuing flow of information and news releases designed to inform and activate voters. No organized opposition to the bond program was apparent, though occasional unfavorable comments were directed toward the parks program because it seemed to some that this furnished a wedge for locally integrated facilities. On the other hand, the Negro population of the county was about 7 per cent of the whole (compared to Atlanta's Negro proportion of 34 per cent) and showed no marked growth or tendency toward residential desegregation.

As of October 1, 1961, 75,373 residents were formally registered for the election. Cynics expected a rather light turnout, however, because local bond elections throughout the nation in the previous decade had stimulated less than 40 per cent of the eligible voters to cast their ballots. Indeed, the Institute of Communication Research at Stanford University found that voter turnout was higher when adverse

TABLE 3

VOTING DISTRIBUTION ON TEN BOND ISSUES
IN DEKALB COUNTY, OCTOBER 10, 1961

Bond Item	For	Against
Incinerator	14,138	3,801
Health center	11,832	5,571
Libraries	12,450	5,675
Fire stations	13,480	4,245
Sewers	12,807	4,937
Water mains	12,595	4,975
Roads and traffic	12,218	5,491
Civic building	9,964	7,515
Parks	10,769	6,854
Airport	9,839	7,727

opinions were strongly felt, particularly in the case of school bond issues. County officials, on the other hand, hoped for a strong turnout, because opposition was neither strong nor organized. On election day, almost 18,000 (or 24 per cent) did find their way to the polls in the county's forty-seven voting precincts. Somehow, this was interpreted by county officials as a "fine" turnout—perhaps because all the bond issues were approved. (See map on page 125.)

Considering the ten issues as a whole, voter support was

about two to one. The smallest majority was given to the airport improvement program and the civic building, while the clearest approbation (3-4 to one) was accorded such unglamorous improvements as the incinerator, fire stations, sewers, and water mains. In general, too, strongest support came from the suburban arc and the Decatur area.

It is, unfortunately, not yet a truism that election *results* are less revealing than the *voters themselves*: their essential characteristics, dominant motives, and the processes by which they arrive at voting decisions. A bond election is a particularly appropriate occasion for analyzing the basic nature of the voting process; it is relatively free of the more dramatic and explosive aspects of elections for *office:* party conflicts, emphasis on personality, defense and criticism of past official behavior, and the like. Consequently, it was anticipated that interviews with a sample of voters would furnish relevant information on three interrelated aspects of voting behavior:

1. What is the role of status and status differences in voting intentions and decisions? Evidence on this matter is extremely mixed, most probably because of differing research designs and the variety of election situations that have been studied. On the other hand, a previous study of voters in the Atlanta area immediately following the 1960 Presidential election demonstrated that voting patterns were most closely associated with occupational differences. But a preliminary analysis of the bond election in DeKalb County revealed a fairly strong relation between status and vote. Three indicators of status were used in this analysis: proportion of persons with eighth grade education or less; proportion of the employed population in blue collar occupations; and pro-

portion of families earning $5,000 or less in 1959.[4] For the county's voters as a whole, using the voting precinct as the unit and vote on the health center as a measure of approval, the rank correlations were as follows:

Vote and index of education   .65
Vote and index of income   .67
Vote and index of occupation   .71

2. What, in fact, are the patterns of exposure to and impact of influence sources on voting decisions? In particular, what are the relative weights of informal personal contacts, official appeals, and various types of mass media? Previous studies indicate that personal influence is more effective than mass media, that the latter principally serve to bolster already formed attitudes and decisions.

3. Finally, since local elections presumably focus on issues that are more likely to be meaningful and "close" to the voter, can we identify the presence and the influence of "community commitment" or "civic responsibility" in voting behavior?

It was anticipated that the most relevant factors or variables in the voting process would not be sufficiently "variable" in the close districts to permit the identification of useful differentials and therefore of adequate *explanations* of voting decisions. Consequently, special attention was given to voting districts with *high* levels of support for the bond program, and those with relatively *low* levels of support (only three districts furnished less than 30 per cent support for specific bond items).

In selecting a sample of voters from these districts, it was extremely important to ensure that the three ecological divisions (urban, suburban, and rural fringe) be given adequate representation. In addition, a total sample size of about 250 voters was decided upon, in view of time and personnel considerations. The sample design was therefore adjusted to give somewhat more representation to urban districts; somewhat less to suburban districts—since the latter would require considerably more travel time for interviews. Since this study was not designed to provide a representative picture of the total county vote—however desirable that might be—but rather of significant segments of that vote, this adjustment did not seem to offer any bias in subsequent analysis and interpretation. But the nature of the sample should be remembered in our later discussions.

Specifically, the sample was chosen in this manner. High and low support voting districts were distinguished by two pools, each subdivided into urban, suburban, and rural fringe categories. From each subcategory, two districts were chosen at random, giving a total of twelve districts in which interviews were to be held. For each district, the official voting lists (i.e., persons who had actually voted) were sampled systematically to provide a predetermined number of interviewees, plus a set of alternates. In each urban or suburban district, 25 voters (plus 10-12 alternates) were picked, while 12 or 13 voters (plus 5-6 alternates) were selected for each rural fringe district.

This projected sample was reduced by the usual difficulties in a study of this kind. The leading difficulty was inability to find the respondent at home (after four or five callbacks), but refusal to be interviewed was a bit higher than expected (about 8 per cent). Other reasons for a reduced sample were: respondent's illness; respondent's moving to a new address, not traceable; and incorrect address on registration rolls. Each source of failure of response was plotted by district and, with one exception, no particular concentration in a specific area or type of area was found. The exception was in the outright refusal category, which was somewhat concentrated in the rural fringe and in southwest DeKalb, adjacent to Atlanta's extension into the county. As far as can be determined, the net result of this reduction was some loss of lower status voters in the final sample of 165 voters.

During the two weeks following the election interviews were conducted by students of sociology and political science. To save time and avoid repetition, only five of the ten bond issues were investigated: the health center, roads and traffic, the civic building, libraries, and parks. Each interview lasted from thirty to forty minutes, with excellent cooperation and generally high interest in the final results on the part of respondents.

A detailed examination of the findings follows in the next three chapters.

CHAPTER 3

STATUS FACTORS
AND VOTING PATTERNS

THE PREVAILING THEORY of social stratification emphasizes the importance of determining relative social position for an understanding of aspects of behavior. The opportunities and limitations encountered by persons at specific status levels also have a direct bearing. A wealth of research seems to support this general contention,[1] but at least two issues remain unresolved. First, which of the available indicators of status difference best explains behavioral and attitudinal differences in a population? As a corollary question, which indicators of status are most useful in understanding specific types of behavior (e.g., child-rearing, mental disorders, voting choice, educational adjustment, and the like)?[2] Second, what accounts for the variable strength of status factors in explaining behavioral differences at different points in time and in different categories of behavior (religious, political, recreational, etc.)? While the present study assuredly cannot present definitive answers to these questions, the findings and analyses here may produce tenable clues concerning the complex operation of status variables in contemporary society.

First, it may be helpful to define the concepts of status and status differences and to explain the choice of status indicators for this study. Essentially, status is a *relative* term, which refers to a degree of responsibility and social worth that are accorded to some category of persons. The crucial feature of status, however, is that a person's conception of his status and the community's evaluation of his status agree with one another. When this is true, social behavior directed toward those in equal, higher, or lower status can be predicted with some accuracy.

Though all status differences in a community cannot be found to form a hierarchical scale, there is a strong tendency on the part of persons, and therefore of the social scientists who wish to understand them, to be more aware of relative or "vertical" status differences. The labels we apply most often to status categories clearly reflect this interest (upper, middle, lower), as do the connotations we attach to such terms as professional, unskilled, businessman and worker, old resident and newcomer.

However, because of the informal and flexible nature of status distinctions in our society, a single, clear, unequivocal mark of status is not practicable. Consequently, the authors have tried to include a representative range of status indicators so as to allow the different facets of status to reveal potential and meaningful differences in voting behavior. The status aspects used in this analysis are popularly and professionally evaluated as important: age, sex, type of residential area, length of residence, income, and occupation. Also, the way in which the voter *subjectively* rated his own status was considered both revelant and potentially significant in explaining "deviant" or unpredicted voting behavior.

The basic hypothesis with which this chapter will be concerned is that acceptance of the bond issues is strongest in the higher income, occupational, and residential categories of county voters. In other words, not only is voting asserted to be positively related to status variables, but it was anticipated that of the various aspects of status studied, the previously mentioned three would be most closely related to voting choice. Occupation, income, and residential area will be focused upon later; the following is a summary of the findings on the remaining status variables:

Sex. On all five issues, women showed somewhat greater support than men, with the strongest difference being in the vote on the civic building.

Age. With the same clarity on all five issues, voters in the 40-60 age group were more favorable to the issues than were younger or older persons.

Previous residence. Under the assumption that one's status is at least partly related to influences derived from type of community experience, voters were classified in terms of their previous residence—urban, suburban, rural. In analyzing the results of this tabulation, it was found that voting was *not* significantly related to differences in the community background of voters.

Length of residence. While there was a tendency for those with shorter residence (under 10 years) in the county to approve the bond issues, length of residence did *not* show a statistically significant relation to voting.

Obviously, the meaning of these patterns cannot be established without examining the effects of other variables. Parenthetically, the connection between age and voting (and to a lesser extent, sex and voting) appears to be an indirect consequence of the character of differential income (see discussion below, p. 57).

MAJOR STATUS VARIABLES AND VOTING PATTERNS

Income. As the accompanying tables testify, support for the bond issues is positively related to income level. There is, in addition, a strong tendency for support to increase with each succeeding income category. Indeed, these differences are also highly significant statistically.

Occupation. The choice of a meaningful scale of occupational categories is a difficult task, one that is always subject to criticism. However, the classification used in this study had already been found to be both manageable and discriminating in an earlier investigation of voting in the Atlanta area.[3] Although the categories should not be considered a completely objective ranking of occupational types, they do provide an acceptable ordering of occupations in terms of skill, responsibility, and socially valued achievement. In descending status order, these categories are: professional and large proprietors, medium management, small proprietors, white collar and clerical, skilled and semi-skilled.

TABLE 4

VOTE DISTRIBUTION BY INCOME CATEGORY ON FIVE BOND ISSUES

A. Health Center

Income Category	For	%	Against	%
Under $5,000	25	65.8	13	34.2
$5,000-10,000	47	72.3	18	27.7
$10,000-15,000	33	91.7	3	8.3
$15,000 and over	20	87.0	3	13.0
	$\overline{125}$		$\overline{37}$	

$$\chi^2 = 8.83$$
$$.02 > p > .01$$

B. Libraries

Income Category	For	%	Against	%
Under $5,000	20	52.7	18	47.3
$5,000-10,000	38	58.5	27	41.5
$10,000-15,000	31	86.1	5	13.9
$15,000 and over	20	87.0	3	13.0
	$\overline{109}$		$\overline{53}$	

$$\chi^2 = 14.26$$
$$p < .001$$

C. Roads and Traffic

Income Category	For	%	Against	%
Under $5,000	22	57.9	16	42.1
$5,000-10,000	42	64.6	23	35.4
$10,000-15,000	32	88.9	4	11.1
$15,000 and over	21	91.3	2	8.7
	$\overline{117}$		$\overline{45}$	

$$\chi^2 = 13.33$$
$$.01 > p > .001$$

TABLE 4 (*Continued*)
D. Civic Building

Income Category	For	%	Against	%
Under $5,000	15	39.9	23	60.1
$5,000-10,000	34	52.3	31	47.7
$10,000-15,000	29	80.6	7	19.4
$15,000 and over	16	69.6	7	30.4
	94		68	

$$\chi^2 = 11.76$$
$$.01 > p > .001$$

E. Parks

Income Category	For	%	Against	%
Under $5,000	19	50.0	19	50.0
$5,000-10,000	39	60.0	26	40.0
$10,000-15,000	26	72.3	10	27.7
$15,000 and over	19	82.6	4	17.4
	103		59	

$$\chi^2 = 8.50$$
$$.02 > p > .01$$

In terms of these five categories, a consistent relation between voting and occupation of voters for any of the bond issues could not be found. Furthermore, even waiving for the moment the assumption that the five occupational categories form a scale, statistically significant differences between occupational categories on four of the five issues are still not obtained. (The exception is libraries.)

Since income proved to be very significantly related to voting choice, it seemed likely that income differences might obscure a potentially meaningful relation between occupation and voting. Consequently, for the health center issue, voting was separately tabulated by high and low income groups for each occupational category. Unfortunately, this method reduced the data in several occupational categories,

TABLE 5

VOTE DISTRIBUTION BY OCCUPATIONAL CATEGORY
ON FIVE BOND ISSUES

A. Health Center				
Occupational Category	For	%	Against	%
Professional and Large Proprietor	39	90.6	4	9.4
Medium Management	27	79.4	7	20.6
Small Proprietor	9	60.0	6	40.0
White Collar	40	75.4	13	24.6
Skilled	11	61.2	7	38.8
	126		37	

$$\chi^2 = 7.22$$
$$.10 > p > .05$$

B. Libraries				
Occupational Category	For	%	Against	%
Professional and Large Proprietor	36	83.8	7	16.2
Medium Management	24	70.6	10	29.4
Small Proprietor	9	60.0	6	40.0
White Collar	34	64.2	19	35.8
Skilled	7	38.8	11	61.2
	110		53	

$$\chi^2 = 7.18$$
$$.05 > p > .02$$

requiring the collapsing of occupations into two divisions. As Table 6 shows, this procedure now yields a modest positive (and statistically significant) relation between voting and occupation. Income differences, on the other hand, seem to have a very slight effect on this relationship. It appears likely that (1) income and occupation are relatively inde-

TABLE 5 (*Continued*)

C. Roads and Traffic

Occupational Category	For	%	Against	%
Professional and Large Proprietor	36	83.8	7	16.2
Medium Management	26	76.7	8	23.3
Small Proprietor	10	66.7	5	33.3
White Collar	38	71.7	15	28.3
Skilled	8	44.5	10	55.5
	118		45	

$$\chi^2 = 4.80$$
$$.10 > p > .05$$

D. Civic Building

Occupational Category	For	%	Against	%
Professional and Large Proprietor	29	67.4	14	32.6
Medium Management	22	64.7	12	35.3
Small Proprietor	6	40.0	9	60.0
White Collar	32	60.4	21	39.6
Skilled	6	33.3	12	66.7
	95		68	

$$\chi^2 = 4.32$$
$$.20 > p > .10$$

TABLE 5 (*Continued*)
E. Parks

Occupational Category	For	%	Against	%
Professional and Large Proprietor	32	74.4	11	25.6
Medium Management	21	61.8	13	38.2
Small Proprietor	8	53.7	7	46.6
White Collar	34	64.2	19	35.8
Skilled	9	50.0	9	50.0
	104		59	

$$\chi^2 = 2.24$$
$$.50 > p > .30$$

pendent of one another in explaining voting patterns and (2) the income variable is a somewhat more helpful predictor of variations in voting in this particular election.

Residential area. Assuredly, area of residence is somewhat less objective and less easily measurable than income and occupation as an aspect of social status. However, taking a metropolitan county as a system in its own right, it seems reasonably clear that prevailing values define suburban residence as most prestigious, while rural or rural fringe residence is accorded least prestige. The status significance of residence in the city of Decatur is not free from ambiguity. Decatur is an old, incorporated community, with the standard range of services for its size. Its more desirable residential areas are adjacent to the highly regarded suburban areas. Consequently, Decatur's over-all status seems to be higher than that of the rural fringe but not quite as high as

TABLE 6

VOTE DISTRIBUTION BY OCCUPATIONAL CATEGORY
AND INCOME FOR THE HEALTH CENTER

Vote	Professional & Proprietor		All Others		Total
For	86	88.7%	40	64.5%	126
Against	11	11.3%	22	35.5%	33
	97	100.0	62	100.0	159

High Income

Vote	Prof. and Proprietor		All Others		Total
For	32	100.0%	21	75.0%	53
Against	0	0.0%	7	25.0%	7
	32	100.0	28	100.0	60

Low Income

Vote	Prof. and Proprietor		All Others		Total
For	54	83.1%	19	55.9%	73
Against	11	16.9%	15	44.1%	26
	65	100.0	34	100.0	99

$$\phi_{\text{Total}} = .289 \qquad \chi^2 = 13.30$$
$$\phi_{\text{High Income}} = .333 \qquad \chi^2 = 6.65$$
$$\phi_{\text{Low Income}} = .295 \qquad \chi^2 = 8.62$$

the suburban zone. One would therefore expect a corresponding ordering of support for the bond issues (i.e., highest in suburbs, followed by Decatur, and then the rural fringe).

The results are largely as anticipated. For all five issues,

residential area is significantly related to voting. And on all
but the health center, the descending order of support is
suburban, urban, and then rural fringe.

Again, the possible effects of income differences were in-

TABLE 7

VOTE DISTRIBUTION BY RESIDENTIAL AREA FOR FIVE BOND ISSUES

A. Health Center

	Urban		Suburban		Other		Total
For	63	88.7%	38	86.4%	30	60.0%	131
Against	8	11.3	6	13.6	20	40.0	34
	71	100.0	44	100.0	50	100.0	165

$$\chi^2 = 16.59$$
$$p < .001$$

B. Libraries

	Urban		Suburban		Other		Total
For	54	76.1%	36	81.8%	25	50.0%	115
Against	17	23.9	8	18.2	25	50.0	50
	71	100.0	44	100.0	50	100.0	165

$$\chi^2 = 13.45$$
$$.01 > p > .001$$

C. Roads and Traffic

	Urban		Suburban		Other		Total
For	57	80.3%	39	88.6%	28	56.0%	124
Against	14	19.7	5	11.4	22	44.0	41
	71	100.0	44	100.0	50	100.0	165

$$\chi^2 = 19.19$$
$$p < .001$$

D. Civic Building

	Urban		Suburban		Other		Total
For	49	70.4%	35	79.5%	19	38.0%	103
Against	22	29.6	9	20.5	31	62.0	62
	71	100.0	44	100.0	50	100.0	165

$$\chi^2 = 19.47$$
$$p < .001$$

E. Parks

	Urban		Suburban		Other		Total
For	49	69.1%	36	81.9%	24	48.0%	109
Against	22	30.9	8	18.1	26	52.0	56
	71	100.0	44	100.0	50	100.0	165

$$\chi^2 = 12.33$$
$$.01 > p > .001$$

vestigated. As indicated in Table 8, within the *high income* category voting differences among residential areas are not significant. Indeed, relatively high acceptance was found in all residential areas. But the voting distribution in the *low income* category is notable in two respects: (1) voting is significantly associated with type of residential area; and (2) it reflects the predicted difference between urban and suburban voters, on the one hand, and rural and fringe voters, on the other. Specifically, it is in the low income rural fringe that we find the greatest resistance to the bond issue. Furthermore, it should be noted that virtually all of the association between voting and residential area ($\phi = .237$) is contributed by the relationship with low income voters ($\phi = .236$). This serves to underscore the central role of income as a status variable in the bond election.

TABLE 8

VOTE DISTRIBUTION BY RESIDENTIAL AREA AND INCOME FOR THE HEALTH CENTER

	Residential Category				
	Urban and Suburban		Fringe and Rural		Total
For	91	85.1%	30	63.9%	121
Against	16	14.9	17	36.1	33
	107	100.0	47	100.0	154

$$\chi^2 = 8.65$$
$$\phi_{Total} = .237$$

	High Income				
	Urban and Suburban		Fringe and Rural		Total
For	47	88.7%	6	85.7%	53
Against	6	11.3	1	14.3	7
	53	100.0	7	100.0	60

$$\chi^2 = 0$$
$$\phi_{High} = 0$$

	Low Income				
	Urban and Suburban		Fringe and Rural		Total
For	44	81.5%	24	60.0%	68
Against	10	18.5	16	40.0	26
	54	100.0	40	100.0	94

$$\chi^2 = 5.22$$
$$\phi_{Low} = .236$$

TABLE 9

DISTRIBUTION OF VOTES ON THE HEALTH CENTER
ISSUE BY PERCEIVED STATUS

	Level of Perceived Status						
	High		Medium		Low		Total
For	36	92.3%	90	75.0%	5	83.3%	131
Against	3	7.7	30	25.0	1	16.7	34
	39	100.0	120	100.0	6	100.0	165

$$\chi^2 = 10.35$$
$$.01 > p > .001$$

Perceived status. This aspect of status was based on responses to the question: "Comparing your family with others
in this county, how would you rate your standard of living
and position? Highest or upper group? Well above average?
Middling or medium group? Somewhat below average?
Other?" The responses were distributed as summarized below, with the distributions of voters by occupation and income for comparison. Since there was no investigation of
the criteria by which respondents rated themselves (that is,
by income, occupation, possessions, education), interpretation of these self-ratings in any detail is difficult. However,
it is interesting to note the high percentage of medium and
above-average status identifications and the extremely low
number of "below-average" identifications. As the comparative distribution suggests, respondents' identifications were
somewhat more in line with occupational differences than
with income differences.

An analysis of voting by the perceived status of voters indicates that there is a strongly significant positive connec-

COMPARATIVE DISTRIBUTION OF SELECTED STATUS CHARACTERISTICS IN THE VOTING SAMPLE

Occupational Distribution		Perceived Status		Income	
Prof. & large prop.	26.0%	Upper	1.8%	$25,000 & over	3.6%
Medium management	20.6	Above average	21.8	$15,000-25,000	10.3
Small proprietor	9.0	Medium	72.7	$10,000-15,000	21.8
White collar	32.1	Below average	2.4	$5,000-10,000	39.3
Skilled	10.9	Other & don't know	1.2	Under $5,000	23.0
Farmers	.6			Refused to state	1.8
Unemployed	.6				

tion, with a generally sharp break between upper and above average status, on the one hand, and the remaining status categories, on the other.

To summarize, of the status variables under investigation, *income* and *perceived status* appear to be most closely associated with acceptance or rejection of the bond issues. Sex and age likewise are of some significance, but it seems likely that age differences in acceptance reflect the concentration of "favorable" age groups in "favorable" residential and income categories. The sample is not sufficiently large to test this accurately, however. The problem then is to account for the relation between status and voting choice. Since this is a complex problem, several theoretically relevant aspects will be examined in the remainder of this chapter and in chapters 4 and 5.

ATTITUDINAL CLUES TO STATUS AND VOTING

It is abundantly clear from research on the relation between status and behavior that while an observer may objectively identify a position or relative status for some category of persons, these persons (1) subjectively interpret their own status and (2) express their "real" or "assumed" status by means of characteristic attitudes, values, and opinions. These personal interpretations of status, it seems, constitute a link between the superficial opportunities and limitations of a given status and the ways in which persons behave in specific situations. Indeed, these attitudinal aspects provide important clues to both the predicted and the unanticipated

TABLE 10 (*Continued*)

E. Parks

Residential Area	Positive		Negative		
	Progress	General or Special Need	Graft	No Need, Don't Know & Other	Total
Urban	24 33.8%	21 28.6%	8 12.3%	18 25.3%	71
Suburban	11 25.0	25 56.9	2 4.5	6 13.6	44
Other	5 10.0	19 38.0	14 28.0	12 24.0	50
	40	65	24	36	165

$$\chi^2 = 24.26$$
$$.01 > p > .001$$

need for the bond issue, fear or mistrust of county officials, no need for the bond item, no answer or "don't know." Clearly, the first two categories are *positive* reasons, while the remainder are *negative* in character. How, then, are these reasons distributed among the status categories in the sample?

As Table 10 shows, there is a statistically significant difference between the different *residential areas* on voting for all five issues. Furthermore, suburban voters were somewhat more motivated by positive reasons than the urban voters, while fringe and rural voters were highly negative in their approach to the health center.

An analysis of the voting reasons among the occupational divisions in the sample shows that the differences are in the expected direction but are too small to be significant. Again, occupation fails to provide a useful tool for predictive purposes. Income, however, is very significantly related to voting reasons, with the higher income groups being more likely to give positive reasons for their votes.

TABLE 11

REASONS FOR VOTING CHOICE ON THE HEALTH
CENTER ISSUE BY INCOME CATEGORY

Income Category	Positive Reasons		Negative Reasons		Total
Under $5,000	25	65.8%	13	34.2%	38
$5,000-10,000	47	72.3	18	27.7	65
$10,000-15,000	33	91.7	3	8.3	36
$15,000 and over	23	87.0	3	13.0	26
	128		37		165

$$\chi^2 = 15.28$$
$$.01 > p > .001$$

Earlier, perceived status was found to be significantly associated with voting choice. But perceived status seems to be variably related to voting reasons. On the parks issue, which was for some voters connected with the desegregation question, voting reasons were predominantly positive for all categories of perceived status. In the case of the more

TABLE 12

REASONS FOR VOTING CHOICE ON THE HEALTH
CENTER ISSUE BY OCCUPATIONAL CATEGORY

Occupational Category	Positive Reasons		Negative Reasons		Total
Professional and Large Proprietor	39	90.6%	4	9.4%	43
Medium Management	27	79.4	7	20.6	34
Small Proprietor	9	60.0	6	40.0	15
White Collar	40	75.4	13	24.6	53
Skilled	11	61.2	7	38.8	18
	126		37		163

$$\chi^2 = 5.16$$
$$.30 > p > .20$$

TABLE 13

REASONS FOR VOTE ON THE PARKS ISSUE
BY LEVEL OF PERCEIVED STATUS

Level of Perceived Status	Positive Reasons		Negative Reasons		Total
High and Above Average	26	66.7%	13	33.3%	39
Medium	75	62.5	45	37.5	120
Below Average and Don't Know	4	66.7	2	33.3	6
	$\overline{105}$		$\overline{60}$		$\overline{165}$

$$\chi^2 = .247 \text{ (nonsignificant)}$$

"neutral" issues (such as the health center), perceived status
was greatly related to reasons for voting choice. There was
a greater tendency for those with above-average perceived
status to supply positive voting reasons, while voters who

TABLE 14

REASONS FOR VOTE ON THE HEALTH CENTER
ISSUE BY LEVEL OF PERCEIVED STATUS

Level of Perceived Status	Positive Reasons		Negative Reasons		Total
High and Above Average	36	92.3%	3	7.7%	39
Medium and Below Average	92	73.5	33	26.5	125
	$\overline{128}$		$\overline{36}$		$\overline{164}$

$$\chi^2 = 12.68$$
$$p > .001$$

TABLE 15

DISTRIBUTION OF ATTITUDES TOWARD PRESENT TAXES BY OCCUPATIONAL CATEGORY

Attitude	Prof. & Large Pro-prietor		Small Pro-prietor		Medium Manage-ment		White Collar		Skilled		Total
Taxes Too High	15	34.8%	9	60.0%	18	53.0%	29	54.8%	9	50.0%	80
Taxes about Right or Too Low	28	65.2	6	40.0	16	47.0	24	45.2	9	50.0	83
	43	100.0	15	100.0	34	100.0	53	100.0	18	100.0	163

$$\chi^2 = 4.95 \qquad .30 > p > .20$$

perceived themselves as having below average status were more likely to employ negative reasons in voting on the health center.

Economic attitudes and status. It may of course be assumed that the relation between status and vote on the bond issues is mediated by differences in economic ideas and attitudes among the status categories in our sample. Thus, people who vote for the bond issue might be expected to be largely uncritical of current tax rates, while negative voters would be predicted to interpret tax rates as excessive. Actually, this expectation was not supported by analysis. Though there was a slight tendency for lower status voters (in terms of income, occupation, and perceived status) to view local taxes as too high, this was not statistically significant. The closest approximation to significance, however, was in the relation of perceived status and attitude to current taxes.

We also examined the possibility that the relation of status

TABLE 16

DISTRIBUTION OF ATTITUDES TOWARD PRESENT TAXES BY INCOME GROUP

Attitude	Under $5,000		$5,000-10,000		$10,000-15,000		$15,000 & Over		Total
Taxes Too High	21	57.9%	36	55.4%	14	38.9%	8	34.8%	79
Taxes about Right or Too Low	17	42.1	29	44.6	22	61.1	15	65.2	83
	38	100.0	65	100.0	36	100.0	23	100.0	162

$$\chi^2 = 5.02$$
$$.20 > p > .10$$

TABLE 17

ATTITUDES TOWARD PRESENT TAXES
BY LEVEL OF PERCEIVED STATUS

	Perceived Status			
Attitude	High or Above Average		Below Average	Total
Taxes Too High	13	33.4%	67	53.2%	80
Taxes about Right or Too Low	26	66.6	59	46.8	85
	39	100.0	126	100.0	165

$$\chi^2 = 5.12$$
$$.05 > p > .02$$

to vote might reflect differences in desired methods of public fund-raising. To discover the preferred method, the following question was asked: "If more taxes are needed for county services in the next few years, what means of raising this money would you favor: sales tax, increased property tax, increased fees or licenses, increased personal property tax, a county income tax, more bond issues, other?"

The results of this analysis are quite enlightening. Neither income, nor occupation, nor perceived status was significantly related to preferred methods of raising money. In general, lower status occupational groups were somewhat more favorable to a sales tax, while upper occupational groups were slightly more favorable to bond issues and secondarily to a sales tax. In terms of income, bond issues were more acceptable to the highest category, with little difference between lowest and medium categories. The sales tax seemed to attract increasing support as voters were located

TABLE 18

ATTITUDES TOWARD RAISING PUBLIC FUNDS
BY INCOME CATEGORY

Income Category	Means of Fund-Raising				
	Bond Issues	Property Taxes	Other Taxes	Don't Know	Total
Under $5,000	7 18.4%	5 13.4 %	22 57.8%	4 10.4%	38
$5,000-$10,000	15 23.0	5 .07	38 58.4	7 10.7	65
$10,000 and over	16 27.1	11 18.6	21 35.7	11 18.6	59
	$\overline{38}$	$\overline{21}$	$\overline{81}$	$\overline{22}$	$\overline{162}$

$$\chi^2 = 6.51$$
$$.50 > p > .30$$

in the lower portions of the income scale. Voters with higher perceived status were more receptive to bond issues than those of a lower status, but the sales tax was fairly well accepted at all levels of perceived status.

Perhaps two conclusions can be drawn. The lack of sharp and consistent differences in economic attitudes among our status categories is quite evident. In addition, voters in most status categories agreed on the desirability of two forms of fund-raising (bonds and a sales tax) and the relative impracticality or undesirability of property taxes, an income tax, or increased fees. This evidence indicates that the values and motives associated with the different voting patterns of our status categories are not primarily economic or utilitarian in nature.

Political orientation. In an election that largely excludes the use of party labels, formal political affiliation cannot be expected to provide useful clues to the association between status and vote. However, the nature of one's political philosophy or basic political orientation seemed to offer some possibilities, especially since political orientation was found to be of some value in Campbell's study of the 1956 Presidential election. To obtain a rough indicator of each voter's political ideology, he was asked:

Which of the following statements comes closest to your personal thinking about politics and government these days?

1. Most of our political problems are really differences between liberal, radical, and conservative ways of managing our public affairs.

2. Most of our domestic and foreign problems can be solved if *one* of the major parties (Democrats or Republicans) really controls our national government.

3. Most of our local and national political problems really are the result of conflicts between business, unions, the farmers, and other types of interests.

4. Regardless of which party is in office, we must have officials who are personally likable, good family men, and without any scandal in their private lives.

5. Improper influence, dishonesty, and corruption play too large a part in our national political affairs.

The first three statements represent various forms of an ideological, partisan, or interest-group orientation. They have in common the evaluation of political affairs through a positive or negative application of some *organized group* or *category*. In contrast, the last two statements appear to approach political affairs through a *personal* and dominantly *moral* set of standards. Parenthetically, the distinction between ideological and personal-moral orientations was used because it seemed to be more in line with a significant dimension in modern life: the relative degree of personal and impersonal participation or commitment in community af-

TABLE 19

POLITICAL ORIENTATION OF VOTING SAMPLE
BY INCOME GROUP

Income Category	Political Orientation				
	Ideological		Personal-Moral		Total
Under $5,000	12	32.4%	25	67.6%	37
$5,000-10,000	21	34.4	40	65.6	61
$10,000-15,000	13	41.9	18	58.1	31
$15,000 and over	12	60.0	8	40.0	20
	58		91		149

$$\chi^2 = 5.08$$
$$.20 > p > .10$$

fairs. The greatly used distinction between liberal-radical and conservative, on the other hand, seemed to demand considerable and undesirable subjective categorization.

In general, differences in political orientation are not clearly related to status differences. On an income basis, there is a moderate tendency in this direction, but it is far

TABLE 20

POLITICAL ORIENTATION OF VOTING SAMPLE
BY RESIDENTIAL AREA

Residential Area	Ideological		Personal-Moral		Total
Urban	22	34.9%	41	65.1%	63
Suburban	20	52.6	18	47.4	38
Rural and Fringe	16	33.3	32	66.7	48
	58		91		149

$$\chi^2 = 3.96$$
$$.20 > p > .10$$

TABLE 21

POLITICAL ORIENTATION OF VOTING SAMPLE
BY OCCUPATIONAL CATEGORY

Occupational Category	Ideological		Personal-Moral		Total
Professional & Large Proprietor	17	41.4%	24	58.6%	41
Medium Management	14	41.1	20	58.9	34
Small Proprietor	5	33.3	10	66.7	15
White Collar	18	33.9	35	66.1	53
Skilled	2	11.1	16	88.9	18
	56		105		161

$$\chi^2 = 11.72$$
$$.02 > p > .01$$

short of statistical significance. Yet this predicted relation is rather clearly indicated when *occupation* is taken as an index of status. When we shift to *residential area,* much of the relation between status and political orientation becomes uncertain. Finally, *perceived status* does not turn out to be

TABLE 22

POLITICAL ORIENTATION OF VOTING SAMPLE
BY LEVEL OF PERCEIVED STATUS

Level of Perceived Status	Ideological		Personal-Moral		Total
High and Above Average	18	50.0%	18	50.0%	36
Medium	36	33.0	72	66.7	108
Below Average	4	66.6	2	33.4	6
	58		92		150

$$\chi^2 = 5.75$$
$$.10 > p > .05$$

consistently or significantly related to basic political attitudes. We must conclude that political attitudes do not adequately explain or elucidate the rather solid connection between voting choice and voter's status level.

CONCLUSIONS

The evidence reviewed in this chapter permits several relatively tenable conclusions that seem to deserve further examination and verification.

1. Several superficial aspects of the status position of voters are probably irrelevant either to prediction or understanding of voting choice in a bond issue election. These status aspects are: length of residence in an area, previous residential location, age, and sex. Though females were more favorably disposed to the bond issue than were males, in general high income was more closely associated with positive votes *among both males and females.* Similarly, while the 40-60 age group contributed the greatest proportionate support to the bond issue, income differences seem to be more important than age *per se.* Thus, all age groups had significantly higher support levels in the high income categories, with the heaviest high income support in the under 40 group and the most decisive low income support in the 40-60 group.

2. Of all the major status variables considered, income, residential area, and perceived status (and perhaps occupation) were found to have modest but statistically significant (and somewhat independent) relations to voting choice. The qualitative classification of status aspects does not permit the use of the usual measures of correlation, but it may

be helpful to indicate the comparative degree of association derived from phi coefficients (based on fourfold classification of data):

Voting and income: $\phi = .23$
Voting and residential area: $\phi = .33$
Voting and occupation: $\phi = .41$
Voting and perceived status: $\phi = .18$

3. Despite the significant association between voting and the above-mentioned status variables, it would be misleading to conclude that status directly affects voting choice. Consequently, an examination was made of the possible role of economic and political attitudes as expressions of status differences. Significantly, these attitudes were *not* consistently related to status differences or to voting. But *reasons* for approving or disapproving the bond issue were rather markedly related to income differences, suggesting that certain status categories perhaps perceived the election in terms of criteria that transcend both their specific status positions and the particular decisions of a single local election.

4. The pattern of these results, in short, suggests the necessity of supplementing the analysis of status with (a) other aspects of the social experience of voters and (b) a consideration of more discriminating attitudinal correlates of status. Consequently, attention should be shifted to the role of influence processes in clarifying the connection between status and voting. Then, in an attempt to satisfy the objective in (b) the significance of "civic responsibility" as an attitude-cluster in local elections will be examined.

CHAPTER 4

COMMUNICATION AND INFLUENCE

THE ELECTION SO FAR has been described as not merely a division between "yes" and "no" votes but also as a reflection of a strong and pervasive difference in *outlook* between two broad categories of county residents. On the one hand was found a willingness to face, and finance some solutions to, problems of growth and expanded service. This attitude is most clearly found in the residents of Decatur and suburban areas, in middle and high income categories, among professionals, large proprietors and managers, among relatively recent residents, and among persons forty to sixty years of age. An opposing viewpoint approaches county government in traditional terms, looking upon it as a necessary evil that should neither be changed nor trusted. This attitude stems fundamentally from an inability to accept the dramatic changes fostered by increasing industrialization, population expansion, and the spread of urban values. Consequently, its adherents have understandable apprehensions about the future and a reluctance to "invest" in a world they have not made and do not admire. Residents of the county's rural and fringe areas, persons with modest incomes, with jobs in skilled or semi-skilled trades, in white collar positions, in farming or small businesses, and often those with longer residence in the county (or previous residence in rural areas) seem to be dominated by this second viewpoint.

THE ROLE OF MASS COMMUNICATIONS IN ELECTIONS

The sources from which the voters gathered information about the bond issue election were investigated during the survey. Most studies of the flow of information during the electoral process have relied upon data collected by means of surveys of voters during an election for public office. Within this context it has been suggested that the voting decision is more a reflection of fundamental social and personal values and that information is received within the framework of these values. Consequently, people may be expected to absorb essentially only that portion of the appeals of mass communication that is satisfying because it reinforces their pre-existing attitudes.[1] On this subject, Paul Lazarsfeld and Robert K. Merton have observed:

For Americans who have been socialized in the use of a toothbrush, it makes relatively little difference which brand of toothbrush they use. Once the gross pattern of behavior or the generic attitude has been established, it can be canalized in one direction or another. Resistance is slight. But mass propaganda typically meets a more complex situation. It may seek objectives which are at odds with deep lying attitudes. It may seek to reshape rather than canalize current systems of values. And the

successes of advertising may only highlight the failures of propaganda.[2]

Examples of the resistance to propaganda have usually been
developed through studies of partisan elections. Partisanship, itself a measure of strong ideological commitment, provides "cues" that enable the voter to evaluate the worth of
information presented through mass media and, in so doing,
insulate himself against potentially disturbing and contrary
points of view.[3] Given the operation of selective perception,
the essential function of mass media is to reinforce or activate latent attitudes; conversion from one viewpoint to another is rare.[4]

Since the effect of mass communication during heated and
controversial campaigns is to excite and intensify partisan
loyalties, what can be said of an election characterized by
low turnout, lack of interest, and no organized presentation
of opposing arguments? On unfamiliar issues might not mass
communications have greater effect, since there usually is no
counter-stimulation of latent attitudes? The possibility that,
in the absence of a clear crystallization of opinion, the impact of short-term impersonal factors might be greater has
been suggested by Carl Hovland: ". . . the elections which
have been studied are typically major ones, concerning
which the public is usually moderately well informed . . . it
is possible that on minor issues and local candidates the effect of newspapers is considerably greater."[5] The bond issue
was indeed a minor one, even by local standards. Compared
with the Democratic primaries that occurred a year later,
the bond issue election was insignificant, if voter turnout can
be assumed to indicate importance. Although the turnout of
17,941 (24 per cent of the eligible voters) was the highest

for bond issue elections in the history of the county, it was small in comparison to the 52,632 votes cast in the primaries.

The Distribution of Information

The officials of the county government went to considerable lengths to obtain support for the passage of the issues but were not met by any organized opposition. Neither the Democratic nor Republican local organizations took positions on the election. Most of the active voluntary associations in the county, such as the Chamber of Commerce and P.T.A., were in favor of the issues, and few voices were raised in opposition. Also, the Atlanta Region Metropolitan Planning Commission engaged in a series of supportive activities such as arranging for luncheons featuring speakers representing the county government. All of this activity generated no expressions of contrary points of view. The election simply did not generate much controversy.

Why this was the case can only be a matter of speculation. It would seem plausible, however, to advance the argument suggested by James S. Coleman that community conflict will usually develop when an important aspect of the community members' lives is affected and when the effect is differential.[6] Certainly the most obviously differential effect occurs when the question of taxes is raised. Normally, tax proposals will affect property holders in one way and those without property in another. In this case, the DeKalb County government was careful to provide almost constant reiteration of the fact that the proposed bond issue involved no change in the tax rate. Further, none of the ten items in the bond issue were to the obvious advantage of some groups and to the disadvantage of others. The single item that most nearly approached this type was the proposal to provide new parks, improve the old ones, and build an eighteen-hole golf course. This single item generated the greatest number of unfavorable votes, and evidence indicates that the fear of integration was a major factor. The fact that DeKalb's Negro population is small, getting smaller, and is politically dormant did not serve to diminish the symbolic salience of the threat. The remainder of the items, if examined with care, may have revealed discrimination against certain income or residence groups, but they were apparently not *perceived* in such a manner.

County government public relations. Within the context of this low-keyed election, the variation in penetration between the various sources of information is interesting. The following list of sources was compiled from answers given to the question: "Where would you estimate you heard most about the bond issue?"

> Atlanta papers (38.7 per cent)
> county papers (24.4 per cent)
> county government publications (10.3 per cent)
> voluntary associations (6.0 per cent)
> radio or television (4.8 per cent).

It can be seen that the only sources making any appreciable impact upon the voters were the newspapers. The penetration of radio and television is quite low, but that is because, in contrast to the growing reliance upon these media of communication (especially television) in elections for public office, those promoting the passage of the issues used other means to convey their messages. However, local civic groups cooperated with the county government in creating publicity.

The county government, under the auspices of its public relations office (known as the DeKalb Research-Information Bureau) published and distributed a series of brochures and pamphlets treating each item in the bond issue with care. One of these, entitled "Bonds for Progress," emphasized the fact that the bond issue would require no tax increases. Yet there seemed to be the fear among negative voters that such an increase was contemplated. Another, more elaborately prepared pamphlet, *Progress and DeKalb,* was printed at the expense of sixteen local financial institutions. However, our evidence suggests that the messages of the DeKalb Research-Information Bureau went unheard. Also noteworthy is the failure of the voluntary associations to penetrate the minds of the voters. It is true that there were no groups organized specifically to oppose or support the bond issue, although there were vague rumblings of discontent, which, under more emotional circumstances, might have crystallized into formal organizations. However, the civic and professional associations of the county, such as the Chamber of Commerce, real estate board, bar association, P.T.A., and Business and Professional Women's Club, did exert a considerable amount of energy in seeking to encourage favorable votes.

While the purpose of this study is not to evaluate community power structure, it should be noted that aspiring politicians in the area consider the support of voluntary associations as vital for electoral success. Whatever may be true in elections for public office, it is apparent that in the case at hand the county officials might have spent their time in more advantageous ways than in the courting of prestigious voluntary associations. Of course, it is possible that the overt opposition of the voluntary associations could have damaged the campaign for the bond issue, and, thus, the efforts of the county politicians did have some value. One cannot ignore the probability that much of the efforts of the voluntary associations were reported in the press and came to the attention of the voters in a second-hand manner. Still, while information may have been transmitted in this way, the origin of the information remained unknown. The voters neither knew or cared what the voluntary associations were saying.

Newspapers. For our purposes, we can classify information sources into two categories: county and non-county. Included in the county sources are the county papers and the publications of the DeKalb Research-Information Bureau. The Atlanta papers are the single non-county source. All other sources may be eliminated because of their negligible penetration. The *Atlanta Journal* and *Atlanta Constitution,* both operated by the same publishing company, have become regionally and nationally famous for their editorial defenses of moderation in segregation questions and their general support of causes unpopular in the South. To rural politicians, the "lying Atlanta newspapers" have become a symbol of the dangers of creeping urbanism. Both Atlanta papers editorialized in support of DeKalb's bond issue, and both devoted a substantial number of column inches to the efforts of the county government to "sell" the issues. The

DeKalb county papers, consisting of the daily *DeKalb New Era* and the weekly *Decatur-DeKalb News,* also supported the issue. Both of these papers naturally devote more space to local news and neither is as thoroughly identified with an identifiable set of values as the Atlanta papers. However, the *DeKalb New Era* is usually on the side of economic conservatism. Since all four newspapers were in agreement on this particular issue, the proponents of the bond issue had, in a sense, monopolized the flow of information. Did the absence of counter-propaganda, when coupled with the unfamiliarity of the voters with the details of the election, raise mass media to the status of a key short-term influence?

DIFFERENTIAL PATTERNS OF PENETRATION

One method of approaching this question is to determine if different kinds of voters received information from different sources. On this subject, the data available from the study of national elections suggest that there is concentration, rather than diversification, in sources of information. Lazarsfeld, Berelson, and Gaudet, in their study of the 1940 Presidential election in Erie County, Ohio, found that "with remarkable consistency, political materials distributed through the various media of communication reached the *same* group of potential voters. The people who were exposed to a lot of campaign propaganda through one medium of communication were exposed to a lot in other media; and those who were exposed to a little in one were also exposed to a little in the others." [7] Our evidence indicates that there were two patterns of exposure that may be called high ex-

posure and low exposure. High exposure voters are those
who indicated that they had followed the news about the
election very closely; while low exposure voters indicated
only a peripheral interest in the news. Those who voted in
favor of the issue were found to be high exposure types, and
those who were opposed were low exposure types. This relationship is shown by Table 23.

TABLE 23

**DEGREE OF EXPOSURE BY VOTE,
IN PERCENTAGES**

	High Exposure	Low Exposure	N
Yes	67.9	32.1	131
No	35.4	64.6	31

$\chi^2 = 9.81$ Yes = Vote for 3 or more items
$p < .01$ No = Vote against 3 or more items

Media choice and support for the bond issue. Having described the positive voters as more highly exposed to information, we now inquire into the possibility of differential
exposure. Recalling the original categorization of sources
into county and non-county, we find that the negative voters
were far more concentrated in their exposure than were
positive voters. The negative voters received most of their
information from the Atlanta papers and very little information from the publications of the DeKalb Research-Information Bureau or the county newspapers. The positive voters
were more receptive to sources originating from *within* the
county. In terms of individual participation, the greater
readership of county sources among the positive voters is in
line with the previous finding showing that these voters

TABLE 24

SOURCE OF GREATEST EXPOSURE BY VOTE,
IN PERCENTAGES

	County Sources	Atlanta Papers	N
Yes	67.0	33.0	100
No	40.4	59.6	42

$\chi^2 = 9.10$ Yes = Vote for 3 or more items
$p < .01$ No = Vote against 3 or more items

were typically high exposure types. It could certainly be said that the Atlanta papers were the most easily attainable source of information, since their distribution in the area is pervasive. Indeed, it would be difficult not to be exposed to information about the bond issue through the Atlanta papers. On the other hand, those who gathered information from a *variety* of sources would have to undertake a more active effort in contrast to the passive role of the negative voter.

Media choice and place of residence. In addition to the more active role assumed by the positive voters, greater receptivity to county sources may indicate some measure of community identification. Willingness to support local bond issues, which was used by William Buchanan as an indication of "purposive voting," and readership of local papers can be taken to mean that those people characterized by this voting and exposure pattern identify with DeKalb County as a discernible unit within the Atlanta Standard Metropolitan Area.[8] Such an argument is developed in Morris Janowitz's book, *The Community Press in an Urban Setting*.[9] Janowitz related readership of community newspapers to length of residence, working and shopping habits, participation in voluntary associations, neighborhood contacts, and attitude toward community. He found that readership of community papers tends to increase with length of residence; that those who were active in formal associations relied more upon local sources; and that those people who felt a sense of community integration were likely to be regular readers of local papers.

Janowitz's study is not concerned with reading habits with respect to a particular issue, and his sample is based upon total, rather than voting population. In any case, no significant relation was found between length of residence, participation in voluntary associations and readership of county sources. On the other hand, we did discover that there was a clear relation between *place of residence* and reading habits. We have seen that the greatest support for the bond issues came from Decatur and the suburbs and that greatest opposition came from the rural and fringe areas. It is also true that readership of county sources is greatest in the city of Decatur, substantial in the suburbs, and slight in the rural

TABLE 25

SOURCE OF GREATEST EXPOSURE BY PLACE
OF RESIDENCE, IN PERCENTAGES

	County Sources	Atlanta Papers	N
Decatur	82.7	17.3	58
Suburbs	50.0	50.0	40
Rural and Fringe	32.6	67.4	46

$$\chi^2 = 28.49$$
$$p < .001$$

and fringe areas. As one progresses inward from the fringes to the core of the county, favorable voting and reliance upon county sources increase.

It could also be argued that the closer one gets to Atlanta or the further one goes into the rural areas, the less becomes the identification with DeKalb County, assuming that voting for the bond issue and reading local sources is a measure of such identification. The inhabitants of the inner portions of the county were inclined toward concern with the status of the county as a discrete unit within the vast metropolitan complex that is Atlanta. This area analysis might also be related in some way to migration patterns. Length of residence did not make much difference in reading habits, as Janowitz found, and as one might have expected. However, much of the migration into the county has occurred in the core of the county, where readership of county papers is high. Migration into the fringe areas has not been as great, and these areas are populated by people with longer residence.

The role of income. Income is another variable that sheds some light on reading habits during the election. DeKalb is a fairly wealthy county as the fact that only 23 per cent of the sample earned less than $5,000 annually indicates. In terms of analysis of the vote, it was found that $10,000 was the break-off point; beyond this income the vote for the bond issue became overwhelming. Similarly, there was a much greater readership of county sources among those voters earning $10,000 or more.

One item of information that does not appear in Table 26 is the extent of the exposure to the two DeKalb County government publications, *Bonds for Progress* and *Progress and*

TABLE 26

Source of Greatest Exposure by Income, in Percentages

	County Sources	Atlanta Papers	N
Less than $10,000	13.1	86.9	76
More than $10,000	60.3	39.7	63

$$\chi^2 = 5.60$$
$$p < .02$$

DeKalb. Since so few people were even aware that such publications had been issued there is little point in subjecting readership of these sources to statistical analysis. Only about 12 per cent of the sample read the eloquent words:

DeKalb County has arrived at a crucial point in its long and dramatic history. The time has come when its citizens must decide its future. Shall we be content with the progress we have made and stand on our present accomplishments? Or shall we keep in step with our neighbors and move on? [10]

This small group of voters is composed almost entirely of those in the upper-income category. One is tempted to speculate upon a greater degree of *rapport* between the county government and the economic "elite," since it appears that the less affluent segments of the population did not fit into a web of established communication with the county government. Not surprisingly, the penetration of county publications was greatest in the "prestige" sections of the county, the suburbs.

Attention might be given to some of the background of the bond issue and the county publications. Beginning in May, 1961 a series of public meetings were held "in an effort to determine the needs and the wants of DeKalb's citizens." [11]

Sixty of these meetings were held and were attended primarily by formal office holders and active participants in civic affairs. With some modifications, the recommendations that emerged from these meetings were incorporated into the bond issue proposal and subsequently into the county publications. Hence, in view of the limited audience of these brochures, it is at least a possibility that those who contributed to the preparation of the literature also served as its audience.

The Effects of Communication

When we deal with the effect of mass communications, rather than their penetration, we must first face the fact that newspapers do not change people's minds. It is generally agreed that, while conversion during an election campaign is a rare phenomenon, such changes in voting intention that do take place are the result of personal influence.[12] The data in this case suggest that this assumption is correct. Only 4.4 per cent of our sample indicated that they had been persuaded to vote differently from their original intention. In every case the direction of a change was from opposition to support, and in every case attribution to a specific discussion with friends or family was volunteered. These voters had exposed themselves more intensely, and their personal discussions seemed to revolve around the merits or disadvantages of a particular aspect of the proposed bond issue. That is to say, they originally intended to vote in favor of *most* of the items, and their discussions convinced them that they should support *all* of the items.

Personal discussions. With regard to personal discussions during the elections, we found that 44.2 per cent of the sample had discussed the proposal with some combination of family, friends, neighbors, and co-workers. The pattern of exposure did not differ significantly between "yes" and "no" voters. In sharp contrast to exposure to mass communications, both groups engaged in conversations in which the subject of the bond issue was raised in nearly equal proportions. Furthermore, the pattern was substantially the same for all districts (Decatur, suburban, rural, and fringe). However, it should be mentioned that rural voters reported the least amount of personal contacts concerning the election, while suburban voters reported the largest amount, a tendency that may be regarded as surprising in view of the presumption that rural life emphasizes personal relations.

In spite of such differences, while personal discussions were more prevalent than exposure to mass media, there was no differentiation as sharp as that which occurred among newspaper audiences. One possible explanation for this lack of variance may be found in the greater salience of personal contacts as contrasted with mass media. The bias of mass media is set by forces external to the individual. He, however, as the receiver of biased content, may consciously or unconsciously weed out unsatisfactory content and avoid hostile sources.[13] Hence, the negative voters avoided the county papers. On the other hand, personal contacts are naturally strongest among like-minded individuals. Robert E. Lane notes that "one reason why political discussion is likely to take place between people who agree with one another is that, like other interaction, it tends to take place in socially homogeneous groups; within the family, within the same occupational strata, and to some extent, within ethnic boundaries." [14] In such situations, the voter would be surrounded by a compatible environment, whatever his values, and no need to indulge in selectivity would present itself. Favorable voters talked with those with whom they agreed, as did unfavorable voters.

Variations among positive and negative voters. While engaging in political discussions during the campaign was the special characteristic of no particular group, the relative importance attached to such discussions does vary significantly. In order to ascertain variations in the effectiveness of the several sources upon various voting publics, the techniques originally employed by Berelson, Lazarsfeld, and McPhee in *Voting* were used. The question was: "Looking back till the time you first heard about this bond election, which of the following do you feel had the most influence on the way you voted?" Choices were: family, friends, or co-workers, organized groups, newspapers and radio, and county officials and county publications. In order to get a more sharply delineated distinction between personal and non-personal sources, the distinction between county and Atlanta newspapers was ignored. Not surprisingly, in view of the pattern of penetration, organized groups were rarely mentioned. Since few voters were even aware of the positions and activities of civic and professional organizations, seldom was there any indication that these groups had been influential. Excluding organized groups, the ranking of the importance of sources for the sample as a whole is: newspapers (38.7 per cent), personal contacts (26.0 per cent), and county officials or county sources (17.5 per cent). However, 17.8 per cent of the sample indicated that *none* of the suggested sources had been helpful; they had evaluated their own position and made up their own minds.

When the sample is broken down according to direction of vote, we find that differences in the ranking of influences appear. For the positive voters, the ranking is in conformity with that of the total sample: (1) newspapers, (2) personal contacts, (3) county officials and publications. For the negative voters, however, the ranking is: (1) newspapers, (2)

TABLE 27

MOST EFFECTIVE SOURCE OF EXPOSURE BY VOTE,
IN PERCENTAGES

	Personal	County Gov't. Pub.	Newspapers	No Effect	N
Yes	33.6	20.1	35.5	10.8	104
No	16.3	20.0	29.1	34.6	55

$\chi^2 = 16.25$ Yes = Vote for 3 or more items
$p < .001$ No = Vote against 3 or more items

county officials and publications, (3) personal contacts. Thus personal contacts played a diminished role among the negative voters, while county sources and publications seemed to be more crucial. Recalling for a moment the discussion of penetration, we observe that the tendency to engage in personal discussions about the election was about the same in both groups. Yet these discussions had greater meaning for those who intended to vote for the bond issue.

The negative image of the county. In the same vein, although the negative voters did not get much of their information from county sources, they indicated that county officials and publications were important, in fact relatively more important than for the positive voters. Taking these two factors into account, our evidence seems to suggest that the personal discussions of negative voters were in the nature of affirmation and reinforcement, a function usually ascribed to non-personal sources. Their discussions did not revolve around the precise issues at stake in the election; rather the election was viewed in general, vaguely defined terms in which the county politicians functioned as symbols of evil. The county government provided hostile symbols around which critical attitudes could be built and maintained. Although the questionnaire had reference to government publications, the negative voters tended to respond in terms of the *personal attributes* of particular county officials, since exposure to publications was slight.

In accordance with their distrust of the county government, the negative voters voiced their belief that the money would be misused. The following selection of comments from these voters illustrates this mistrust: "The tax payers are getting robbed." "Why build parks for Negroes? When you get it built, the Negroes move in and close it." "This is too much money to lose on irresponsible characters." "This is too damn much money to give S. O. B. politicans." "In the last bond issue they promised not to increase taxes, but they did." Also characteristic of the negative voters was a tendency to relate a certain aspect of the bond issue to personal gain. Hence, negative voters in Skyhaven, which is on the south side of the county immediately adjacent to the Atlanta city limits, believed that the bond issue was promoted for the benefit of the wealthier portions of the county to the north.

While both positive and negative voters attributed about equal importance to county sources, they did so for sharply divergent reasons. County sources were important to the negative voters because they excited a pre-existing attitude of distrust. What was said or not said in these sources was of minimal importance. "They" might go to great lengths to stress the promise that the issue would involve no tax increase, but "they" were not to be believed. With these firm attitudes, the inclination of negative voters to maintain that *no* sources were of importance becomes more understandable. Starting with the assumption that "anything the county government is for, I'm against" does not leave much room for persuasion or enlightened evaluation.

The neutralization of any potential effect of county propaganda by pre-existing hostile attitudes can also be discovered by looking at differences in ranking of sources by income and area. The tendency was for higher income groups to be much more sensitive to personal discussions but to be only slightly more influenced by county officials and county propaganda than lower income groups. These same sources were thought to be about equally important in the suburban areas, which gave heavy support to the bond issue, and in the rural areas, which gave considerably less support.

Conclusions

Joseph T. Klapper suggests, ". . . sources which the audience holds in high esteem appear to facilitate persuasion, while sources which the audience holds in low esteem appear to constitute at least a temporary handicap." [15] In this case, two distinct groups perceived the same source—the county government—in a decidedly different manner. The perception of the source, which the voters carried into the information absorption process, determined to a considerable extent the direction of the reinforcement. To the negative voter, the county sources were indeed useful, not because they supplied information that contributed to an evaluation of the issue to be decided, but because they provided symbols for the strengthening of hostile attitudes. For the positive voters, the same sources dissipated possible doubts on specific aspects of the election. In either case, a basic thread of the study is extensive immunity to argument, information, or persuasion. Both sets of voters followed their own preconceived notions of their own and the county's needs. It is true, however, that the resistance to information is more characteristic of the negative voters with their firmer "set" of attitudes.

The persistence of selective perception. Even in a low turnout, nonpartisan election, the social group memberships of voters serve to provide the "cues" that activate strongly ego-involved attitudes—a function that is attributed to political parties in national elections. The deeply rooted differences in outlook between the two categories of voters, which were crystallized in the perception of the county government, thus were brought into play even though the issues were unfamiliar. The role of mass communication in this kind of election does not appear to be materially different from its role in heated, partisan elections; its persuasive capacities are sharply reduced by the attitudes of those who are exposed. Given the fact that this low-interest election did not create a situation in which non-personal sources were maximized in terms of influence, patterns of readership did vary according to the type of voter.

Community identification. The county–non-county dichotomy can be used to provide a measure of community identification. Certain discrete portions of the county population indicated by their reading and voting that they are "involved" with DeKalb County, to some extent identifying their personal well-being with that of the community. The concentration of this group of voters in the wealthier suburban and Decatur districts calls to mind the argument of Robert C. Wood, who said that suburban voters are inclined to "care" more about their community.[16] Indeed, it is in these areas that the county government found its greatest support and in these areas where its appeals were most heeded and least needed. These "newer" portions of the county—those areas that have grown rapidly in population in the past twenty years and those areas that attract families in urban-centered occupations—have committed themselves to local and county development, to optimism in community affairs. These areas do not appear to be populated by those who fit the stereotype of the "escapist" suburbanite or urban fringe dweller who is alleged to have little interest in his surroundings and likewise to favor low taxes and limited public spending.

This kind of election, with its low turnout, attracted voters primarily from the "normal" areas of support. This fact suggests that those persons who were not inclined to support community projects were not activated into overt opposition. Although the publicity program of the DeKalb County officials was designed to interpret financial and administrative changes to their more conservative constituents in such a way that these changes would not be defined as threats or invasions of old value systems, it operated to crystallize opposition from the tradition-oriented areas of the county. If the propaganda attending the election had been more pervasive, it is quite likely that its penetration would have been in the hostile areas. If, in their efforts to inform, the county officials had induced sufficient stimulation for controversy to increase turnout, the increase in voting may well have been accounted for by negative voters. In one sense, then, the failure of the county government to reach more than a small fraction of potential voters, despite prodigious amounts of appearances and speeches in the weeks preceding the election, may have contributed to the success of the election.

Coleman's comments upon fluoridation controversies have bearing on the above point. He finds that the higher the turnout, the less the chance of a fluoridation measure passing: "Ordinarily, in city-wide elections, turnout is low, consisting primarily of the most active, interested citizens, those most *attached to* community affairs . . . when an issue becomes heated, creating a large turnout, the vote results would include a larger component of persons uninvolved in and unattached to community affairs." [17] If the population growth of the county continues in its present direction, the "attached" voters will increase as a proportion of the total voting public, thus making it likely that increasingly solid support for county improvements will be forthcoming. The county government has been forced to operate as an intermediary between the unattached areas and those areas that demand modern public services and increased public spending. As the balance of power and support shifts permanently to the urban-oriented parts of the county, this role will become decreasingly necessary. Just as the bond issue election was a result of the needs of the urban and suburban areas of the county, county officials in the future will be increasingly impelled to represent to a large extent the most expensive needs and interests of the "metropolitan" additions to DeKalb's population. They will have to develop and maintain continuous contacts with the urban-suburban nucleus of support.

CHAPTER 5

CIVIC RESPONSIBILITY
AND VOTING PATTERNS

IN TRYING TO understand voting behavior, social scientists
are moving from ecological determinism toward a consideration of more "subjective" factors. One such factor is the way
a voter defines his role in the political process, including the
obligation or identification he feels toward his immediate
community. To the extent that this obligation has been expressed by means of working in elections, voting regularly,
and participating in civic organizations, it has become the
object of social science research to an extensive degree.[1]
However, while ecological and attitudinal variables have
been related to various types of political participation, there
has been little investigation of the *meaning* of political activities to those who engage in them. Specifically, although
the phrases "political obligation," "citizen duty," and other

variations have often appeared in political science literature, relevant studies have dealt with these phenomena as
though they were dependent variables and not as factors
that might explain differences in the direction of the vote.

A major exception is the work of Campbell, Gurin, and
Miller, in which the authors discover an attitude that they
call "sense of citizen duty." Citizen duty consists of "the
feeling that oneself and others ought to participate in the
political process, regardless of whether such political activity is seen as worthwhile or efficacious." [2] Sense of citizen
duty is most prevalent among those with high income and
education, but even when these factors are held constant
there is a clear and positive relation between citizen duty
and political participation. Thus, those who participate do so
because it is their obligation and not necessarily because
they expect reward, the authors conclude. While stating that
political obligation has consequences and is not solely a function of ecological variables, the authors still assume that a
quantitative evaluation of participation in political or civic
affairs is the best single measure of citizen duty or civic responsibility, without inquiring into possible differences in
mode of participation.

Students of local behavior have been prominent in seeking out evidence of the kind of responsibility described by
Campbell, Gurin, and Miller, and they have added a new
dimension, place of residence. In particular, Robert C. Wood
points to the "ideal type" suburbanite as one who differs
from residents of the central city in his "acceptance of an
obligation for extensive civic participation. . . ." [3] Wood believes that this acceptance is a form of escapism. The desire
to avoid the partisan politics of the core city, manifested in

a fiercely independent or aloof attitude toward national politics, is translated into an intense identification with the suburban community and an inclination to be zealously concerned with local affairs. Wood thus employs the notion of
community identification to explain a pattern of political activity. In a similar vein, Zimmer and Hawley found that residents of the fringe areas of Flint, Michigan, knew and cared
little about local politics and could not act in a "construc-
tive" manner toward problems.[4] Here again the location of
a person within a particular geographical area is found to
be of significance.

Although place of residence appears to account for some
variance in attitude toward the local community, it surely
cannot be the best single predictor of attitudes. Is it not
likely that social areas tend to develop into homogeneous
units containing essentially the *same* socio-economic status
types? Would it not be likely, then, that social background
is a more reliable key to the understanding of perceptions
of the community? In particular, it does not seem proper to
talk about the suburbanite as though this designation in itself provides a description of an exclusive pattern of behavior.

Such is the opinion of Scott Greer, who has developed a
typology of suburban participation types. He points to a gen-
eralized identification with the suburban community as
manifested in resistance to proposals for merger into a
larger metropolitan community, a desire for the preservation
of the smaller suburban system, and a wish to remain aloof
from a larger more depersonalized political community. Yet
he does not maintain that all suburbanites are alike in the
intensity of their desires.

There are three distinct types of participation in the local society of suburbia; (1) Community Actors, who are involved in the larger local community, (2) Neighbors, who participate only in the small-scale world of the neighborhood, and (3) Isolates, who have no role in either kind of social structure.[5]

Community Actors, says Greer, are most likely to vote in local elections and be well informed about local affairs. Neighbors may be expected to be less involved; while Isolates are "generally outside both the communication flow and the action that takes place on the local scene."

As we would expect, the Community Actors are over-represented in the upper-status neighborhoods. They are well educated, and they make a good income from prestigious occupations. Thus we can distinguish among suburbanites both in terms of their socio-economic status and the variations in behavior that correspond to differences in status. Greer also maintains that the variable *urbanism* independently affects participation; the greater the urbanism, the less the participation, reading about local news, and "caring" about local politics.[6]

Presumably, the variations in behavior patterns reflect variations in underlying attitudes toward the local community. Thus one would speculate that the Community Actors are likely to be the local "progressives" and contribute their energies toward the improvement of the community. This kind of assumption can not be made simply by noting the greater participation among certain types of local actors, but must inquire into the *manner* of participation and the *meaning* of such participation. For example, why does the Isolate remain outside the local political system? If he *does* occasionally participate, is it probable that his participation will take a different form from that of the habitually active person? Such questions can be best approached from the theoretical perspectives of Robert K. Merton—specifically, his treatment of *anomie*.[7]

Anomie, a feeling of normlessness or rootlessness, was originally used to describe the condition of a social system. However, Merton was most concerned with using the term to describe an *individual* state of mind. He argued that this condition is most commonly produced because of the existence of goals (usually socially defined) without access to the means for achieving these goals. In a sense, anomie and frustration can be equated. Most important, anomie and its consequent feeling of isolation do not necessarily produce withdrawal but may contribute to certain forms of "deviant" behavior, for example, "active" participation. Rebellion, in fact, can be produced by alienation from "reigning goals and standards."[8]

Merton's idea of anomie has proved useful for students of local government and politics. Clearly, the local community could serve as a symbol for the hostilities of anomic individuals if only because it is more immediately available to their consciousness. We have already noted the tendency of upper-income groups to support local reform. It is also expected that there will be proportionately fewer anomic individuals in the upper-income groups.[9] It seems fairly clear that persons living in low economic and social status neighborhoods will be more personally demoralized than those in higher income and social status neighborhoods; and that anomic individuals will tend to remain isolated from the patterns of local politics. Such individuals will be more likely to feel that community leaders are indifferent or hostile to their needs; and they, in turn, will be hostile toward community leaders.[10] Lacking the sources that provide a buffer against personal defective integration, the anomic individuals will interpret local politics in terms consistent with their feeling of being "left out." Therefore, it is of course quite likely that anomie in the low socio-economic groups of a community contributes to the low participation of these groups in local politics. However, it is also possible that the participation of such groups, *when it does occur,* will be in the nature of a negative reaction against the perceived hostile system from which the lower status groups exclude themselves.

Participation is not in itself a necessarily satisfactory measure of civic responsibility, because the reasons for such participation may be "irresponsible." The intention here is not to impose personal values upon the motives of voters, but rather to suggest that some people may vote a certain way for reasons that have little or no relation to the issues in an election. For example, there is a difference between a person who votes against a school bond issue because he feels there is a more urgent need to build an auditorium and a person who votes the same way because he believes that local politicians are trying to get rich by raising taxes. Such a difference is implied by Murray Levin's reference to the "alienated voter" and William Buchanan's description of attitudes exhibited by the "purposive voter." [11] In both studies there is the suggestion that the type of vote is related to a sense of identification with the community. The purposive voter feels he has some control over the content of community decisions, while the alienated voter does not feel that he "belongs." Consequently, the alienated vote is likely to be an expression of distrust or a striking out at what is perceived to be the in-group of local politics, while the purposive vote reflects a more cognitive appraisal of community needs. Thus Buchanan, for example, feels that a vote in favor of a local waterworks bond or the officials who supported it is a purposive vote. Corroborative evidence is provided by Coleman's analysis of fluoridation referenda. Coleman suggests that the ordinarily low voter turnout in city elections is indicative of the continued participation of the citizens "most attached to community affairs." [12] Consequently, if a high turnout occurs, the increase in vote is drawn from normally uninterested persons. Such persons are most likely to vote *against* measures sponsored by the local administration but would be stimulated to do so in relatively few instances. A large vote, indicating the mobilization of unattached citizens unleashing their frustrations by a negative vote, usually results in the defeat of fluoridation.

Assuming, as do the authors cited above, that support of community programs is correlative with a sense of civic obligation, further exploration of the kinds of social characteristics that are most likely to be productive of this attitude is in order. To accomplish this, civic responsibility may be defined in terms of (1) the direction of the vote and (2) the reasons for the vote. In an urban context, people who vote for programs that are perceived to provide needed improvements in the community are said to have civic responsibility. Civic responsibility is consequently expressed in a willingness to accept the obligation to support community endeavors that are necessary for the establishment or maintenance of a satisfactory level of public service. These persons identify their own well-being with that of the community and are willing to assume increased financial responsibility; whereas those without (or with a lesser degree of) civic responsibility are likely to resist programs that they believe will increase their financial burdens. The voter who exhibits the traits of civic responsibility will not only vote favorably on community programs but also will have "responsible" reasons for so doing. Such reasons are distinguishable from those based primarily upon emotional or intuitive factors (such as distrust of the motives of local officials who are supporting improvement programs) and are characterized by frequent reference to "community need," "local progress," or similar phrases.

In Chapter 3, an analysis of positive votes on specific bond issues enabled us to discover several patterns that are relevant to the understanding of civic responsibility. The salient findings from Chapter 3 may be briefly indicated at this point for convenience:

1. Taking each of the five bond issues separately, level of support is positively related to income level of the voters. In other words, the higher the income the greater the approval rate for each issue.

2. Occupational differences among voters appear to be questionably related to levels of support. Indeed, a *significant* relation between voting and occupation only emerged when we collapsed the occupational categories. Furthermore, income differences had no noticeable effect on the relation between voting choice and occupation. Consequently, we concluded that occupation was not a particularly useful category in interpreting the patterns of voting in this election.

3. In general, area of residence shows a very significant

relation to voting. On four issues (only the health center provides an exception) the greatest proportionate support was in suburban areas, followed by urban areas, and with lowest support in rural fringe areas. Significantly, there was little difference in voting decisions among high income voters in these three types of residential area. But among *low income* voters, rural fringe areas tended to view each of the bond issues negatively, while urban and suburban areas were more favorably disposed.

4. For each of the five bond issues, voters who interpreted their relative status as above average or higher were more likely to vote positively than those whose perceived status was reported to be below average.

If one were to accept the contention that these proposals for physical items and services are intimately connected with the continued development and improvement of the county, then it would be justifiable to pursue one aspect of civic responsibility in DeKalb County. It seems reasonably well established that the major locus of civic responsibility is found in voters (1) from suburban areas, (2) with above average incomes, (3) with medium or higher occupational status, and (4) with above average perceived status. In addition, civic responsibility (as reflected in positive votes on single issues) is most evident among voters in the 40-60 age group and among relatively recent residents—each of whom probably enjoys above average income and/or suburban residence. For this county and this election, then, civic responsibility somehow reflects the experience of persons who possess or pursue comparatively high status positions and who seem to be favored with some degree of upward social mobility.

Consistency of support. A particularly sensitive indicator of civic responsibility may be found in the voter's attitudes toward the *composite* of bond items. Of course, consistency in voting choices in a given election is not in itself evidence of high civic responsibility. Straight party voting, for example, reflects consistency, but it is not likely that a high degree of civic responsibility is likewise involved. On the other hand, the character of the issues in the bond election (and more specifically of the five issues on which we have focused)

TABLE 28

CONSISTENCY OF SUPPORT FOR THE BOND
ISSUES BY RESIDENTIAL AREA

Support Level	Urban		Suburban		Other		
All Five Issues	39	54.9%	32	74.0%	18	36.0%	89
Two-Four Issues	18	25.3	6	13.0	12	24.0	36
None or One Issue	14	19.8	6	13.0	20	40.0	40
	71		44		50		165

$$\chi^2 = 15.00$$
$$.01 > p > .001$$

enables us to make the assumption that the greater the approval for all the bond issues, the greater the degree of civic responsibility among voters. Employing a practical distinction among three levels of consistency, our task is then to (1) locate characteristic levels of support for the various status categories and (2) compare these findings with the previously noted patterns of civic responsibility.

As Tables 28, 29, and 30 indicate, consistency of support is significantly related to type of residential area, income level, and occupational category. Among residential areas,

TABLE 29

CONSISTENCY OF SUPPORT FOR THE BOND
ISSUES BY INCOME LEVEL

	Under $10,000		Over $10,000		
All Five Issues	49	47.5%	38	66.2%	87
Two-Four Issues	20	19.4	15	25.4	35
None or One Issue	34	33.1	6	8.4	40
	103		59		162

$$\chi^2 = 10.68$$
$$.01 > p > .001$$

consistency is proportionately higher in suburban areas and lowest in rural fringe areas. Consistency of support is appreciably higher in the higher income categories, with disproportionately low amounts in the "none or one" category. Similarly, though with comparatively less clarity, consist-

TABLE 30

CONSISTENCY OF SUPPORT FOR THE BOND
ISSUES BY OCCUPATIONAL CATEGORY

Support Level	Prof. & Large Prop.		Medium Management & Small Prop.		White Collar & Skilled		
All Five Issues	26	59.0%	26	53.0%	36	51.4%	88
Two-Four Issues	14	31.8	10	20.4	11	15.6	35
None or One Issue	4	9.2	13	26.6	23	33.0	40
	44		49		70		163

$$\chi^2 = 9.96$$
$$.05 > p > .02$$

ency of support is highest in professional and large proprietor groups, lower in the manager and small proprietor group, and lowest in the white collar and skilled worker group.

Furthermore, both length of residence and age were significantly related on consistency in voting. Greatest consistency was found among recent residents (who, as we have previously noted, tend to be in higher income categories and in suburban areas) rather than long-term residents. Voters in the 40-60 age category proved to be the most consistent in positive voting, while the oldest voters (60 and over) were least consistent.

Clearly, the data on single issues and on the composite of five issues indicate that civic responsibility is principally located in a socially homogeneous category, marked by relatively recent residence, early middle age, and higher than average economic and occupational positions.

Attitudinal correlates. In Chapter 3 the relations between several status variables and attitudinal items were explored in the attempt to clarify the importance of status in the vot-

TABLE 31

CONSISTENCY OF SUPPORT FOR THE BOND
ISSUES BY LENGTH OF RESIDENCE

Support Level	Under 10 years		10-20 years		Over 20 years		
All Five Issues	37	71.1 %	18	40.9%	34	49.2%	89
Two-Four Issues	5	.09	12	27.2	19	27.5	36
None or One Issue	10	19.2	14	31.9	16	24.3	40
	52		44		69		165

$$\chi^2 = 11.50$$
$$.05 > p > .02$$

observed. First, the multiple correlation of voting and these status variables is rather modest (.43), indicating that a very large portion of the variance in these data remains unexplained. The square of .43 is 18 per cent, meaning that 82 per cent of the variance in vote cannot be explained by these status variables. Second, the character of the relation be-

A Hypothetical Model of the Relation of Civic Responsibility to Social and Psychological Structures

tween civic responsibility and status variables is by no means self-evident. It would be misleading to conclude, for example, that the economically favored citizens vote "responsibly" because they can afford the present and future expenses of approved new or extended county services.

Perhaps account can be taken of these necessary reservations by suggesting a theoretical model that incorporates the present data and also the basic orientation of modern social psychology. As the data suggest, status variables seem to provide *potentiality* for acquiring and maintaining attitudes related to our conception of civic responsibility. While the theoretically expected connection between high status and vote was found, there were also a considerable number of "deviant cases," which suggest that voting and status are either somewhat independent or, more likely, related by means of intervening variables. These variables seem to be *attitudinal*. Perhaps a very important component is the voter's conception of community needs and his "commitment" to the community. The crucial problem at this point is explaining both the *social sources* and the *supports* for such attitudes.

It may well be that the *relation* between civic responsibility (and its attitudinal correlates) and status characteristics depends upon different *types* of commitment to the community and, likewise, upon different but sincerely held conceptions of community needs. Civic responsibility, from this standpoint, might then be defined not in universal terms but as a reflection of community types. In traditional rural communities, for example, the dominant conceptions of order, fear of change, thrift, and limited governmental operation are allied with a sense of civic responsibility that is personal, immediate, and limited in range. By contrast, in expanding, urbanized areas, the acquired insistence on extensive and more efficient community services (both public and private) creates a revised ideal of civic responsibility that is clearly uncongenial to the rural conception. Briefly, the "urbanized" conception seems to emphasize active citizen support of progressive change, greater efficiency, and willingness to raise and apply public funds for desired public services.

Though adequate information of this score is not yet available, it would appear that civic responsibility is subtly transmitted to typical members of various status categories by characteristic community agencies (mass media, churches, schools, and key influentials). In traditional rural communities there tends to be high consensus among status categories on the rural responsibility pattern, perhaps because of the relative absence of competing conceptions (or their organized expression). On the other hand, in rapidly urbanized areas, such agencies as the mass media and schools purvey the urban conception of civic responsibility, with perhaps more success to higher-status categories because these persons tend to be more regularly exposed (or disposed) to these agencies. (It is a moot question at this point whether these influences serve primarily as *sources* or *supports* of civic responsibility.)

If the hypothesis is valid, the voting differences between high status persons in urban and rural areas may then be understood, and differences between low status persons in

TABLE 33

DISTRIBUTION OF POSITIVE VOTES ON THE
HEALTH CENTER, BY OCCUPATION AND
RESIDENTIAL AREA

Residential Area	Occupational Category			
	High		Low	
	Actual	Expected	Actual	Expected
Urban	32	31.7	29	29.2
Suburban	26	19.7	12	18.2
Rural and Fringe	9	15.4	21	14.4
	67		62	

$$\chi^2 = 14.38$$
$$p < .001$$

TABLE 34

DISTRIBUTION OF POSITIVE VOTES ON THE
HEALTH CENTER, BY INCOME AND
RESIDENTIAL AREA

| Residential Area | Income Category | | | |
| | High | | Low | |
	Actual	Expected	Actual	Expected
Urban	23	24.9	32	30.9
Suburban	24	15.7	12	20.2
Rural and Fringe	6	13.1	24	16.8
	53		68	

$$\chi^2 = 18.79$$
$$p < .001$$

urban and rural areas are clearer. These differences probably reflect different community conceptions of civic responsibility. As the accompanying tables suggest by comparisons of actual and expected frequencies of positive votes, high-status persons vote as predicted (or more so) in suburban and urban areas but considerably less so in rural areas. Yet lower-status persons vote as predicted only in urban areas; less than predicted in suburban areas. Somehow, income and occupational differences operate more consistently in urban than in rural or suburban areas in the sample.

One might also point to the possible effects of *selective migration* and *selective retention* in clouding the relation between status variables and "urbanized" civic responsibility. In the urban portion of the sample, no great discrepancies were found. However, in suburban areas there may well have been selective migration of (1) the more "responsible" higher status persons and (2) the less "responsible" lower status persons. On the other hand, the patterns in rural areas present difficult problems of interpretation. While an attempt may be plausibly made to explain the lower-than-expected positive vote among high-status ruralites as a result of emigration of ruralites with urbanized attitudes, the vote among lower-status ruralites simply can not be accounted for as a consequence either of (1) immigration of "responsible" lower-status persons or (2) out-migration of "irresponsible" lower-status persons.

In short, the relation between status and civic responsibility seems to be provisionally traceable to antecedent socialization processes, which transmit conceptions of community needs to social and ecologically distinguishable categories. Only a series of replicative studies will enable anyone to assess the conclusion that status factors are *necessary* or that attitudes toward community are *sufficient,* in producing local voting patterns.

CHAPTER 6

SUMMARY AND IMPLICATIONS

THIS STUDY OF the bond issue election in DeKalb County was
undertaken to explore some of the major factors associated
with differences in voting behavior. A basic assumption—one
that is increasingly shared by students of voting—is that the
act of voting is a culmination of a complex process-series of
implicit and explicit attitude formations and decisions. Consequently, the factors studied were selected for their presumed relevance to the antecedent decision-making processes, which tend to be obscured by the final act of voting.
Specifically, the aim was to assess the discriminatory power
of three kinds of factors in a local, nonpartisan election, and
to examine the extent to which approval or disapproval of
the bond issues could be explained (or clarified) by differences in (1) status levels of voters, (2) exposure to and effects of personal and impersonal influence, and (3) under-

lying attitudes or commitment to the county as a meaningful entity.

To pursue these objectives, it was decided not to merely select a representative sample of county voters, since such a sample would probably not focus upon factors necessary to establish criteria for measurement. Instead, a random sample was selected from the voting lists of districts with either high or low support for the bond issues. The major findings may be placed in three categories:

STATUS VARIABLES AND THE VOTE

1. Greatest support for the bond issues was contributed by voters in the 40-60 age group, with somewhat more favorable rates among females. However, these patterns seem to be largely dependent on the relation between income and voting.

2. In general, approval of the bond issues was highest in the high-income categories, lowest in the low income groups.

3. While detailed occupational differences were not significantly connected with voting, voters in professional, large proprietor, and managerial positions were more likely to support the bond issues.

4. The highest support was found among suburban voters, followed by urban, and then rural fringe voters. Among high-income voters, however, residential differences were not important, since all three residential types provided comparably high levels of support. In low-income categories, on the other hand, approval rates were highest among suburban and urban voters.

5. Voters with above-average perceived status (which tended to be more in keeping with occupational than income levels) contributed higher levels of support than those with below average perceptions of status.

6. Neither length of residence in the county nor the voter's previous residential location was related to approval or disapproval of the bond issues.

7. In general, positive reasons for voting (emphasizing progress and perceived need for improvements) were most often given by voters in suburban and urban areas, while negative reasons were predominantly supplied by rural fringe voters. Furthermore, positive reasons were most concentrated in the upper-income categories.

8. Neither occupation nor perceived status showed a consistent relation to reasons for voting, though there was a slight tendency for those with above average perceived status to supply more positive reasons.

9. Not one of the major status distinctions among voters (income, occupation, residential area, or perceived status) was useful in distinguishing marked differences in attitudes toward current tax rates (and presumably, of different degrees of acceptance of or hostility to added expenditures).

10. Similarly, none of these status distinctions could be clearly related to preferred methods of raising public revenues.

11. With one exception, status differences among county voters are not traceable to differences in political ideology or philosophy. Only the higher occupational categories seem to accept the existence of interest groups as a focal issue in political affairs, while the lower occupational categories tend to take a more personal-moral attitude toward government.

INFLUENCE PATTERNS: EXPOSURE AND EFFECTS

12. Generally, apart from the newspapers, voters reported limited exposure to mass media or personal contacts concerning the bond election.

13. Among those voters who were exposed to mass media, those who reported higher levels of interest and more continuous exposure were more likely to vote for the bond issues than those with lower exposure and interest levels.

14. Likewise, voters who were exposed to more variety of mass media tended to vote favorably in the election. Specifically, positive voters were more likely to read county newspapers and public brochures (in addition to the Atlanta papers); while negative voters tended to read only the Atlanta papers (with which they strongly disagreed, by the way).

15. Exposure to county papers—a useful discriminator of voting choice—was highest among suburban and urban (Decatur) voters, least evident among rural fringe voters. However, such exposure was not related to either length of residence in the county or participation in voluntary associations.

16. Exposure to county papers and to county pamphlets on the bond issue was highest among upper-income categories of voters (and among positive voters as a group).

17. Reported effects of exposure to mass media were quite anemic. But the few instances of change in attitude were all from opposition to approval.

18. Personal influence was reported in similarly substantial proportions among residential areas and as between positive and negative voters.

19. Personal influence was more widespread than exposure to mass media concerning the election. Furthermore,
voters who approved the bond issues indicated that personal
influence was more important as a source of information and
opinion than the ranking reported by negative voters. Indeed, negative voters seemed to form and sustain their decisions from their hostility to specific county officials.

CIVIC RESPONSIBILITY

20. Assuming that civic responsibility could be properly
defined as acceptance of the bond issues and an accompanying commitment to future needs of the county, it was found
that these attitudes were most prevalent in suburban and
Decatur voters, among high-income voters, among those
with above-average perceived status, and among upper-oc-
cupational categories.

21. Another aspect of civic responsibility (the voter's support of the bond issue "package") was likewise most evident
in voters from suburban areas, those in high-income categories, relatively recent residents, those in the 40-60 age
range, and those in the highest occupational categories.

The over-all patterning in these findings suggests that objective and subjective status differences provide an initial
polarization in the county's voters—one that is largely un-
affected by the paraphernalia of mass media or the subtle
influences of informal personal interchange. However, it is
quite clear that status differences alone do not "explain"
voting differences. Apparently, the attitudes basic to our
concept of civic responsibility are not a *consequence* of

above average status (however measured) but a reservoir of values to which high-status voters have considerable access. Yet evidence of substantial (though lesser than among high-status voters) civic responsibility among lower-status voters cannot be ignored. It seems likely, therefore, that differences in voting may be traced to socializing agencies (persons and organizations) both in the cultural milieus of the county and from external sources—each or both of which create and sustain a relatively unique guiding image that is translated into verbal form and into such behavioral choices as voting and selection of mass media.

In fact, the underlying sentiment of the negative reaction to the bond issue (suspicion of county government officials and institutions) is undermined when voluntary associations, mass media, and community leaders come out in support of a local referendum. The absence of reinforcement from such sources leaves the voter without cues and he falls back upon his inherent oppositional tendencies. Any rallying point would heighten the force of these negative sentiments. Consequently, the absence of organizational activity either for or against the issue (to the extent that such activity made an impression on the voters) probably left the negative voters with few institutional restraints upon their desire to express hostility, which they did by voting against the bond issue.[1]

From the various tabulations we have presented, and from the verbatim remarks of the voters in our sample, we can tentatively distinguish two socio-political divisions in De-Kalb County. One such division consists of the recently developed western third of the county, in which are located the city of Decatur, the northern industrial suburbs, and an irregular but rapidly filled-in arc of residential suburbs. This rough segment is largely urban-oriented, regardless of income and occupational differences; its population is to a great extent committed to community growth and expansion of services, and it has tremendous optimism about the future. While many families in this segment are mobile (they are likely to move out or be transferred within the next five years) they do not seem to be either withdrawn or irresponsible with respect to local affairs. Indeed, they demand modern services, efficient government, and foresight and imagination on public issues.

By contrast, in the eastern and southern portions of the county lives a population that maintains a traditional, rural approach toward the world and its intrusive issues. Largely composed of rural, rural fringe, and distant small-town areas, this segment of the electorate appears to view population expansion, increasing industrialization, and the spread of urban values as dramatic changes to be resisted or at least delayed. Families of this persuasion have understandable apprehension about the future, and this is reflected in a reluctance to "invest" morally or financially in a world that they do not understand or control.

Several problems in voting behavior are intimately related to the character of results presented in previous chapters.

1. Is there any meaningful relation between voting patterns in the bond election and voting in state and national elections?

2. If the voting patterns in our sample are clarified by consideration of status differences and levels of civic responsibility, does this enable us to deepen our understanding of the amount, distribution, and social characteristics of nonvoters?

3. What needed revisions in the study and interpretation of *suburban voting* may be reasonably derived from our analyses of the bond election?

PATTERNS OF PARTISANSHIP

We have previously called attention to the "neutral" nature of the bond election and the absence of any discernible activity on the part of organizations that normally engage in political activity. However, this by itself tells us very little about the nature of the response to the bond election on the part of population groups with pre-established reactions to partisan or interest-group-sponsored campaigns. The first chapter contained comments on the available evidence suggesting certain patterns in the relation between local and national votes; we observed that high-status "Republican" groups were more likely to support community reform measures. It was also reported that the degree of competition in an election seems to have an impact on the extent to which local voting patterns coincide with national patterns. With regard to status variables, both the survey data and the analysis of aggregate county data strongly suggest that De-Kalb County is no exception to the rule of high-status support for local reforms.

In regard to the relation between the bond election and other elections held in the area, three such elections were considered: the 1960 presidential election; the 1962 Democratic primary for United States representative; and the 1962 general election for the same office.

In view of the conclusions suggested by other observers, it was expected that there would be a tendency for supporters of Richard Nixon to vote for the bond issues. However, no such relationship appeared. The presidential election was extremely close in DeKalb, with John F. Kennedy winning by less than 1,000 votes out of 46,000 cast. Application of the Spearman rank correlation technique showed that the correlation between support for the bond issues and support for Nixon was only .39. A slightly higher correlation (.42) was found between support for Kennedy and bond issue support. This, of course, tells little about DeKalb's voters.

If this sample is analyzed to try to obtain a clear understanding of local and national patterns, it is extremely difficult to distinguish positive from negative voters on the bond issues by means of their votes for presidential candidates. As Table 35 shows, *both* positive and negative voters in the bond election were Kennedy supporters primarily. While there is a tendency for positive voters to support Kennedy and oppose Nixon, the difference is not statistically significant. Therefore, the conclusion is that there is no discernible relationship between the bond issue vote and the presidential vote. In terms of national party identification, it seems, local Republicans are not necessarily the "progressives."

TABLE 35

DISTRIBUTION OF VOTES ON THE BOND ISSUE
AND THE PRESIDENTIAL ELECTION

| Presidential Vote | Bond Election | |
	Yes (%)	No (%)
For Kennedy	65.6	59.5
For Nixon	34.4	40.5

$$\chi^2 = .78$$
$$.50 > p > .30$$

Turning now to the election for United States representative, the aggregate data are suggestive of a slightly clearer relationship. To understand this relationship, some information on the election and the area might properly be presented at this point.

DeKalb County is in Georgia's Fifth Congressional District, together with Fulton County (including Atlanta) and Rockdale County (rural in character). The district is perhaps the most "politically" constructed in the United States. In order to combat the "malicious" influence of urban areas, the Georgia General Assembly combined urban Atlanta, suburban DeKalb, and rural Rockdale into one district. Furthermore, the recently abolished county unit system virtually assured that the representative from the district would not be chosen by Atlanta, which has a clear majority of the population. This system allocated to each county two "units" for each representative in the lower house of the General Assembly. Because the system of apportionment discriminated against urban areas, Fulton County had three representatives and six unit votes, DeKalb (with considerably less population) had the same number, and Rockdale had one representative and two units. Elections were, therefore, won on the basis of unit rather than popular vote. In effect, this meant that a candidate who carried DeKalb and Rockdale could win, even while losing the popular vote.

This was precisely the case with Representative James C. Davis, who on two occasions lost the popular vote but carried DeKalb and Rockdale. Davis was the "ideal" southern legislator. He was vigorously segregationist, opposed to foreign aid, to federal aid for education, to urban renewal, and he had a consistent record of opposing the Democratic ad-

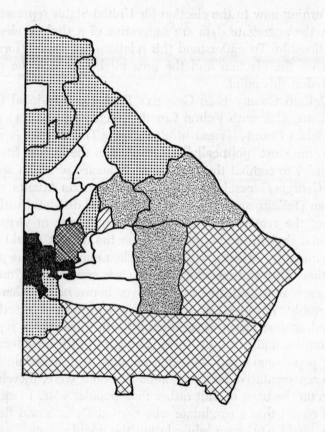

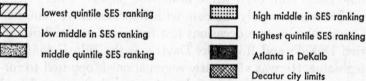

	lowest quintile SES ranking		high middle in SES ranking
	low middle in SES ranking		highest quintile SES ranking
	middle quintile SES ranking		Atlanta in DeKalb
			Decatur city limits

Socio-Economic Status Differences in DeKalb County, 1960

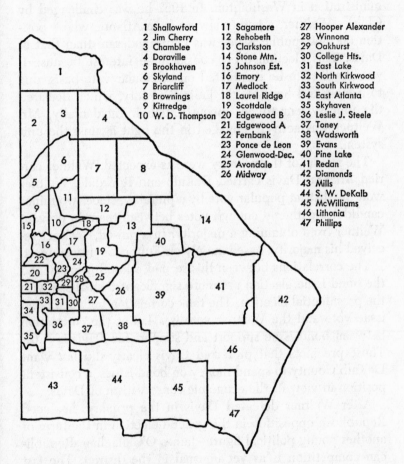

1 Shallowford	11 Sagamore	27 Hooper Alexander
2 Jim Cherry	12 Rehobeth	28 Winnona
3 Chamblee	13 Clarkston	29 Oakhurst
4 Doraville	14 Stone Mtn.	30 College Hts.
5 Brookhaven	15 Johnson Est.	31 East Lake
6 Skyland	16 Emory	32 North Kirkwood
7 Briarcliff	17 Medlock	33 South Kirkwood
8 Brownings	18 Laurel Ridge	34 East Atlanta
9 Kittredge	19 Scottdale	35 Skyhaven
10 W. D. Thompson	20 Edgewood B	36 Leslie J. Steele
	21 Edgewood A	37 Toney
	22 Fernbank	38 Wadsworth
	23 Ponce de Leon	39 Evans
	24 Glenwood-Dec.	40 Pine Lake
	25 Avondale	41 Redan
	26 Midway	42 Diamonds
		43 Mills
		44 S. W. DeKalb
		45 McWilliams
		46 Lithonia
		47 Phillips

Voting Precincts in DeKalb County, 1961

ministration in Washington. In 1962 he was challenged by
Charles Weltner, a young lawyer from Atlanta, whose position on most public issues was more moderate than that of
Davis. This election drew considerable interest because it
was the first to be conducted on a popular vote basis, due
to a long and hard-fought judicial victory, which declared
the unit system to be unconstitutional. Incidentally, Mr.
Weltner was actively engaged in the fight against the unit
system.

The results of the primary were as expected. Weltner carried Atlanta; Davis carried DeKalb and Rockdale. Weltner
won the district popular vote by a plurality, since two minor
candidates gathered enough votes between them to prevent
Weltner from obtaining a majority. In a run-off, Weltner received his majority, based mainly on Fulton County support.

The correlations between this second, run-off primary and
the bond issue election are more significant than those with
the presidential election. The rank correlation between bond
issue vote and the Weltner vote is .34. But the correlation
between bond issue support and support for Davis is − .61.
Those precincts that preferred Davis clearly did *not* want
DeKalb County to spend money on bond issues, a consistent
position in view of the economic conservatism of Davis.

After Weltner defeated Davis in the primary, he faced
Republican opposition in the general election in the form of
another young political figure—James O'Callaghan. Republican competition is as yet unusual in the district. The last
serious opposition was in 1956 and in this instance the Republican candidate was running in the general election more
to avoid the unit system (which applied only to Democratic
primaries) than to present a uniquely "Republican" plat-

form. In the case of O'Callaghan, the situation was quite different; O'Callaghan was supported by a growing number of urban businessmen who sought to establish two-party competition. In the general election, Weltner carried De-Kalb County by a very slim margin. In this case, the correlation between bond issue support and a Republican vote is higher than in the Presidential election. The O'Callaghan—bond issue correlation is .51, while the Weltner—bond issue correlation is a surprising − .26.

These results indicate that the bond issue election was probably more closely integrated with local rather than national politics. The clearest relationship is not based on partisanship, however. The highest correlation with bond issue voting was with voting in the Democratic primary; the next highest in the general election for representative, and the lowest in the Presidential election. In addition, if we divide the DeKalb precincts into groups according to their support for the bond issues and compare these groups on their average percentage of support for the various candidates mentioned above, our previous rank correlations are corroborated. The precincts in the "lowest" ranking supported Davis at a 64.5 per cent level; those in the "highest" category at a 48.3 per cent level. In the general election, the respective percentages of support for O'Callaghan are 42.5 and 51.9. In the Presidential election, the *difference* in support for Nixon between the lowest and highest bond issue precincts is slight: 49.2 per cent as against 52.3 per cent.

By separating precincts into two extreme groups, one can analyze in more detail the relationship between the bond issue and the congressional election. In the first group are precincts that were hostile to the bond issue; in the second are the precincts that supported the bonds. Such a categorization is, of course, arbitrary in some degree. Since there were ten issues in the election, it was decided to group those precincts that had voted against four or more issues. Consequently, this category ranges from precincts that voted against four issues (East Lake and North Kirkwood), to those that opposed eight (Phillips, Diamonds), to East Atlanta, which opposed all ten issues. In the second group, were included only those precincts whose approval rate for all ten issues was 63 per cent or higher. All other precincts were excluded from the following comparison.

The table shows quite clearly that the negative precincts were, with a single exception, urban and rural fringe, with relatively low socio-economic indices. In regard to the Weltner-Davis runoff primary, these precincts without exception preferred Davis by rather impressive margins. In the general election, when the issue of Republicanism was raised, these same precincts showed a tendency to adhere to traditional loyalties. While they much preferred Davis over his more moderate opponent, seven of the eight precincts voted for Weltner in the general election. Despite the fact that O'Callaghan sounded very much like Davis in his public speeches, the appeal to traditional "Democracy" could not be shaken.

In the eleven precincts that make up the high support category, this trend is to some extent reversed. The Davis vote in these precincts was substantially lower than that of the precincts that opposed the bond issue. Davis carried only four of the eleven precincts, in each case by less than 60 per cent of the vote. Actually, only in Avondale did Davis achieve a decisive margin. Again, the general election affords a contrast between these two groups of precincts. In-

TABLE 36

COMPARATIVE LEVELS OF SUPPORT FOR DAVIS
AND WELTNER IN PRECINCTS FAVORING OR
OPPOSING THE BOND ISSUES

Precinct	Area	Composite SES Index	Vote for Davis (Primary)	Vote for Weltner (General Election)
Low Support of Bond Issues				
East Lake	Urban	66.8	63%	51%
North Kirkwood	Urban	63.1	65	58
Southwest DeKalb	Fringe	44.6	76	47
Skyhaven	Suburban	64.1	60	62
Redan	Fringe	38.8	74	57
Phillips	Fringe	44.6	83	51
Diamonds	Fringe	36.3	65	71
East Atlanta	Urban	59.1	64	62
High Support of Bond Issues				
Laurel Ridge	Suburban	87.1	49	35
Ponce de Leon	Urban	57.1	48	48
Emory	Suburban	84.7	42	55
Fernbank	Suburban	84.7	50	46
Johnson Estates	Suburban	85.3	32	63
Skyland	Suburban	72.8	42	45
Medlock	Suburban	86.5	52	42
Jim Cherry	Suburban	73.7	36	46
Avondale	Suburban	76.6	59	41
Winnona	Urban	80.6	54	48
Scottdale	Fringe	52.1	49	62

deed, Weltner carried only three of the eleven high bond support precincts.

One can see that the precincts with a pattern of voting for the bond issue, for the moderate Democratic candidate, and for the Republican candidate in the general election are (with the exception of two precincts) suburban and have a relatively high socio-economic index. In view of the role of Republicanism in the Fifth District and the South in general, such a pattern may be taken to suggest an adherence to more experimentation and change among suburban, high-status areas. However, 1962 was the first evidence of any stable Republican organization; and its appeal was based partly on opposition to the traditional, rural "red-neck" dominance of the Democratic Party. In a sense, then, support for the bond issue and Republican voting may be viewed as representing consistent attitudes in favor of progress; while opposition to the bond issue and adherence to traditional Democratic ties might well indicate a desire for the maintenance of the *status quo*.

NON-VOTING

The survey data of this study are drawn from a sample of the *voting* population. Thus nothing has been learned about the differential features of voters and non-voters. One would expect, from previous research, that those who were motivated to vote in the bond election would be of higher status than those who did not vote. However, if we use the *precinct* rather than the individual as the unit of analysis, there is only a very slight relationship between turnout and socio-economic status. For the county as a whole, the turnout was 24.2 per cent. Of course, there was considerable variation in turnout throughout the county. What are the differences between areas of high and low turnout? For example, the rank correlation between turnout and socio-economic status is .22, hardly indicative of a substantial source of difference. To compare high and low turnout areas, precincts were divided into two groups: those precincts whose turnout was 30 per cent or more and those precincts whose turnout was 20 per cent or less. Table 37 summarizes the results.

Clearly, there is not much difference in the socio-economic status of these groups of precincts. Note, for example, that the precinct with the highest turnout (McWilliams with 39 per cent) and the precinct with the lowest turnout (Edgewood A with .03 per cent) have nearly identical indices of socio-economic status. Likewise, the average socio-economic index of the high-turnout category is 64.7, while that of the low-turnout group is 61.9.

Turning to the matter of the socio-geographical distribution of high- and low-turnout precincts, the evidence does not clearly point to the suburbs as areas of high interest in local politics. Indeed, it seems that precincts located at the boundaries of the county have a higher rate of participation. Of DeKalb's 47 precincts, 23 may be classified as suburban, 13 as rural fringe, and 11 as urban. Seven of the 13 fringe precincts are in the high-turnout group, while six of the 23 suburban precincts are in this group. The most consistent of the geographical patterns is found in the urban category. The five precincts with the lowest turnout are urban, and only one out of 11 urban precincts is in the high-turnout group.

In contrast to the sharp variations in the voting preferences of the three areas of the county, turnout is not related to geographical divisions, except in the case of the urban precincts. In addition, we find the lack of any significant

TABLE 37

Comparison of High and Low Turnout Precincts on Vote for the Health Center and Socio-Economic Index, DeKalb County

Precinct	Area	Turnout	Health Center Vote	Composite SES Index
High Turnout				
McWilliams	Fringe	39.0	68%	44.8
Laurel Ridge	Suburban	38.5	81	87.1
Shallowford	Fringe	38.1	64	71.0
Diamonds	Fringe	35.3	44	36.3
Fernbank	Suburban	34.6	81	84.7
Sagamore	Suburban	33.5	73	88.3
Redan	Fringe	33.1	47	38.8
Phillips	Fringe	32.8	38	44.6
Decatur-Glenwood	Urban	32.3	70	71.7
Clarkston	Suburban	32.2	57	53.9
Southwest DeKalb	Fringe	32.1	42	44.6
Wadsworth	Fringe	31.7	74	74.1
W. D. Thompson	Suburban	31.6	71	88.3
Avondale	Suburban	31.2	77	76.6
Low Turnout				
Doraville	Suburban	20.7	74	69.1
Evans	Fringe	20.0	58	54.6
Brookhaven	Suburban	19.9	73	72.5
Skyhaven	Suburban	18.8	49	64.1
Lithonia	Fringe	18.7	68	41.6
Skyland	Suburban	16.2	78	72.8
East Lake	Urban	14.8	55	66.8
Johnson Estates	Suburban	14.1	87	85.3
North Kirkwood	Urban	11.8	55	63.1
Edgewood B	Urban	11.7	59	68.0
East Atlanta	Urban	11.4	47	59.1
South Kirkwood	Urban	11.3	60	47.3
Edgewood A	Urban	.03	56	43.0

correlation between turnout and direction of vote. Using the vote for the health center as the unit of analysis, the rank correlation between turnout and favorable vote is .08. The average support for the health center among the high-turnout precincts is 61 per cent, for the low-turnout precincts 62 per cent. This is contrary to expectations, since we have previously noted the relationship between turnout and vote in some studies and the finding that often local issues have a greater chance of success if turnout is low. This is based on the assumption that an increase in turnout would be accounted for primarily by voters whose participation is sporadic and whose attitudes are negative. It could, therefore, be argued that low-turnout areas would provide the greatest support for the bond issues in this election. Such an argument is not necessarily tenable because there is simply no way of estimating or predicting the areas from which the "added" voters would be drawn. This, of course, does not deny that a heavier turnout might have reduced the approval rate or even may have defeated many of the bond issues.

In brief, it is probable that the bond election somehow attracted the higher-status individuals from each of the areas of the county, since the median family income of the sample is considerably higher than that of the county as a whole. It is, therefore, possible that increased turnout would have lowered the average economic status of the voters and of a sample selected in accordance with our procedures. It seems likely that, since turnout was exceptionally low throughout the county, only the interested and active citizens actually went to the polls. These "actives" seem to have been distributed about equally in the county. Had turnout been higher, the correlation between turnout and direction of vote might have been more pronounced. The survey data show that individuals in border and other peripheral areas (such as Atlanta in DeKalb) were most likely to oppose the bond issues. It is also true that if we examine the border areas included in the accompanying table, their support is slightly lower than such areas as a whole, especially in the low socio-economic border precincts. In the high turnout category—with the exception of McWilliams, a low socio-economic area with a high positive vote—the low socio-economic border areas voted negatively. On the other hand, these precincts in the low-turnout category generally supported the bond issue. In these areas, at least, low turnout seems to accompany positive voting, but no such pattern emerges for the other types of precincts. One might argue from these data that the most important variables in understanding local participation would be those that reflect the voter's definition of his relation to the community or county. Although this definition might be linked to his residential location, perhaps more explanation of differences in voting could be derived from psychological variables than from status variables.

SUBURBAN AREAS AND VOTING PATTERNS

The dramatic expansion in suburban populations since World War II has provoked an understandable interest in suburban politics and voting behavior. As already mentioned (page 15), there are as yet very few studies of specific suburbs and even fewer studies of suburban voting. In general, the *emerging* conclusions inspired by previous investigations are that (1) there is some variety in the social composition of suburban areas and (2) the novelty or special character of suburbs—as distinct from comparable urban segments—has been rather exaggerated by popular and academic stereotypes. Indeed, one of the most persistent notions about suburban residents is that they are politically quiescent, escapist, and reluctant to accept economic responsibility for local public services. Likewise, on a national basis, it is widely believed that suburban residence creates (or at least bolsters) political conservatism and an affinity for Republican candidates.

Before the relevance and meaning of the DeKalb bond election for the problem of suburban voting can be interpreted, it is necessary to recognize that there is some variation in defining "suburban area." In general, however, suburbs are initially described in *ecological* terms, i. e., in terms of their complex socio-geographic relations to the central city. We may define suburbs as:

. . . those *urbanized nuclei* located outside (but within accessible range) of central cities that are politically independent but economically and psychologically linked with services and facilities provided by the metropolis. By urbanized nuclei we mean those areas outside the central city that have relatively substantial population densities, a preponderance of nonrural occupations, and distinctly urban forms of recreation, family life, and education.[3]

In applying this definition to DeKalb County and its component census tracts and voting precincts, of course, difficulties of interpretation inevitably arise, particularly in distinguishing *suburban* from *rural fringe* areas. It was helpful to assign the suburban label to county precincts with the following features: comparatively dense population; populations with growth rates above the county's rather high rate, areas with little or no farms or without substantial undeveloped acreage, areas within 15-50 minutes' driving time to central Atlanta. Only the city of Decatur possesses most of these "suburban" features, but it is distinguished by its rather static population, a long corporate history, and the fact that it is the largest single population center in the county.

The suburbanite's prominence in support of the bond issues in the voting sample has already been detailed. How does this compare with the situation in the total electorate? Once again for convenience, attention was focused on the health center issue. A comparison of types of voting precincts—urban, suburban, and rural—reveals the following average levels of support:

Suburban (23 precincts) 70.4%
Urban (11 precincts) 61.9%
Rural (13 precincts) 57.3%

These results corroborate the order of support found in the sample, despite the fact that the sample was not designed to be representative of the whole body of voters. In addition, most of the suburban precincts clustered around the average suburban approval rate—in the upper 60's or low 70's—indicating that the independently applied suburban label was quite reliable. However, a comparison of high approval suburban precincts (71 per cent and over) with low approval suburban precincts (60 per cent or under) seemed to point to the importance of socio-economic differences. Consequently, the suburban precincts were compared with the highest and the lowest socio-economic scores. The average approval rate for the former was 73 per cent, for the latter 60 per cent.

These results for the entire voting population of the county seem to indicate two crucial characteristics of suburbanites, at least in a large, rapidly developing southern metropolitan area. First, as a category, suburbanites appear to be in the vanguard of citizen support for various local improvements, for realistic fiscal policies in line with improved services and facilities, and for a strong, progressive *county* government, rather than an emphasis on village, town, or small urban government.

Second, there is some variation in the thinking and voting of suburbanites. Though the suburban portion of our sample is not large enough to permit adequate comparisons, people who live in suburban areas are drawn from a substantial range of income levels and occupations. In addition, as an earlier investigation of the suburban arc in DeKalb County suggested, suburban families may be characterized by differences in style of life.[4] For example, suburban families seem to follow different commuting patterns, variations in participation in formal or voluntary groups, different friendship patterns, and even different types of family goals.

In fact, there is some evidence for the relation between suburban family type and voting change or stability following the move to the suburbs. For example, families who seem to use the suburb as a lever for upward social mobility show a decided shift from Democratic to Republican voting. Suburban families that are highly committed to the suburb and who have a continuous history of participation in voluntary groups seems to have predominantly Democratic back-grounds, but there is only a slight net shift to the Republi-cans following a suburban move. By contrast, families in the suburb that have either internal conflicts about social ob-jectives or that have largely withdrawn from earlier social participation either tend to continue a pattern of non-voting or shift to the Republicans.[5] In short, suburban residence encompasses a broader range of values, attitudes, and politi-cal motivations than the popular stereotypes would suggest.[6]

Whither Voting Research?

During the past thirty years or so, voting research has been marked by a quest for leading patterns and master variables. This has been a difficult task, not only because American society is rather extensive and heterogeneous but also because vast socio-cultural changes have continually altered the nature of an intricate political structure and its relation to other institutions in modern society. Conse-quently, the earlier methods in voting research, with their emphasis on official voting distributions and ecological cor-relations, provided gross clues of a highly selective nature. Thus, the most frequently used variables were geographic location, occupation, income, political affiliation, and religion.

Not till the introduction on a grand scale of survey re-search and the use of scientific samples was the traditional picture of voting challenged by (1) greater concern for vot-ing as a social process; (2) the identification of crucial atti-tudes; and (3) the prominence of troublesome deviations from the major regularities expressed in neat charts, graphs, and correlation coefficients. As a result of these latter emphases, voting studies of the past twenty years have repeatedly identified what may be called the *theoretical trio* of voting analysis: socio-economic status in its various objective and subjective forms, influence and persuasion processes as a source of either maintenance or change of political orientations, and a complex set of primarily non-ideological attitudes that reflect alienation from or commitment to social environments from the neighborhood to the nation. The study of the bond election in DeKalb County is, of course, largely dependent on our interpretation of this emerging tradition in voting research.

But as a review is made of other voting studies, as well as this one, a gnawing question persistently arises. In what ways can we substantially increase our explanation of recurrent variations in voting, within a given election and in any meaningful series of elections?

It is becoming more and more evident that the voter must be studied as a complex social person, whose various facets are inadequately represented by a focus on the voting role alone. From the standpoint of the individual, voting is an infrequent process; it may be said to *punctuate* the equally (or more) absorbing stream of social situations which shape and reflect not only individual personalities but social types. If man is a political animal, as Aristotle and others rightly assert, he finds his "politics" wherever human groups operate, not only in government and public affairs. Consequently students of voting behavior are constrained to examine the ways in which the citizen slips the needle of personality through the arbitrarily delimited fabrics of family, occupation, and religion.

The trio of status, influence, and community commitment
—as commonly used—seems to provide a prerequisite orientation to voting analysis; it ushers us into the anteroom but
not the sanctum. Perhaps this approach is limited because
one tends to employ these variables in practical isolation
from one another, exhausting one before turning to another.
But these three facets can be more fruitfully exploited by
considering the subtle though meaningful bonds that link
them into a distinguishable emergent: *style of life*.

Style of life may be defined as the subjective but shared
manner in which individuals and families appraise and use
the opportunities and limitations to which they are exposed.
This means in practice that similarity of income, occupation,
and so forth does not ensure similarity in meaning or behavior. This principle has been illustrated in the limited
correlations between voting and status and between voting
and exposure to mass media and personal influence. Even
involvement in the community is not predictable on the basis
of type of community alone but also on various group experiences that affect the direction and intensity of commitment.

Voting behavior is in some respects analogous to consumer
behavior as studied by the economist. In recent years, the
presumably objective variable of income has been analyzed
into two components.[7] On the one hand, there is the more
easily measurable current or short-term income of family
units—transitory income—which is subject to the vicissitudes
of income windfalls and reduced employment. Yet, on the
other hand, economists have begun to identify a personally
meaningful conception of "normal" or expected family income—also called permanent income—which is implicitly ap-

plied to an extended time period by the consumer. Significantly, this second component of family income provides a more adequate explanation of consumer expenditure (e.g., on housing) than the first component. Thus, a breadwinner with a current income of $9,000 may follow a scale of expenditures "appropriate" to an income of $7,000 until he alters his conception of "normal" income in line with his revised fortunes. Similarly, among families with incomes above the current subsistence level, there are some whose current income is exceeded by their conception of "permanent" income. The result is "deficit spending," which could not be predicted by knowledge of current income alone.

In the case of voting, perhaps status position and exposure to influence patterns may be regarded as the "transitory" component. Style of life, the complex of crucial attitudes and values by which resources and facilities are judged, may constitute the "permanent" component that is more decisively connected with voting choice in some sequence of elections. Of course, difficulties immediately arise when we try to translate style of life into researchable dimensions. However, it seems clear that some experimentation and courage are in order if one is to develop (1) valid and reliable indicators of style of life that (2) significantly increase our ability to explain problematical variations in voting.

In addition to the traditional lines of thinking and investigation, at least three methods of apprehending politically relevant styles of life deserve further exploration.

1. *Voluntary group affiliations.* Social participation in various organizations and groups outside the family, job, and church is an increasingly important aspect of modern man's

experience. Whether style of life determines or is developed by the pattern of such affiliations is not at issue at this point. More important is the probable effect of distinguishable styles of life on perceptions of voting and on the issues embodied in specific campaigns. Considerably more attention must be paid to identifying styles of life and to the processes by which each style of life channels typical motives and perceptions of the voting role. This problem is closely related to the focus of interest in the so-called "sociology of knowledge," [9] but both specialties must translate guiding assertions into detailed investigations.

2. *Achievement needs.* The recent and very promising research on achievement needs or aspiration patterns has developed another facet of style of life that clarifies ethnic group and class differences, as well as differential national responses to technological and economic change.[10] Though level of aspiration has been studied by a generation of social psychologists, the achievement scale developed by McClelland offers a handy means of measuring differing levels of motivation, which may be used to distinguish voting patterns in an electorate.

3. *Ideological and related factors.* While various voting studies have emphasized the strength of primary group affiliations and socio-economic status in voting decisions, it is by no means clear that voting is totally immune from non-rational value-patterns or ideologies. In fact, the well received thesis of Boorstin that the "genius of American politics" lies in a lack of ideologies can only be accepted if we first agree on an extremely narrow definition of ideology.[11] If ideology refers only to a formally explicit justification of group interests and actions, then few people may be said to

possess ideologies. However, such a definition compels us to ignore widespread existence of ideological clues which are sometimes consonant with, sometimes tenuously related to, objective status positions of voters. Such clues in the form of "themes" or reasons for voting for the bond issues, interest group vs. personal-moral political orientations, racial attitudes, and hostility to public officials were previously reported.

But a systematic analysis of the presence and operation of rationalizations, stereotypes, implicit group goals, and unexamined explanations of experience—ideological elements, in short—is a major necessity in a careful study of any group or social category. It is particularly required in the case of voters because they are called upon to make decisions of a complex nature despite a limited factual base. The discrepancy between knowledge and the need to act is in fact a fertile source of ideological creations. It is, therefore, suggested that style of life can be at least partially inferred from the characteristic viewpoints, myths, and prejudices that voters hold on such matters as: economic affairs, racial and ethnic relations, the legitimate functions of government, the value of formal education, the essential character of specific political parties, the purchase and use of consumer goods, and religious differences and their significance. This listing is exploratory, but it is hoped that additional clues will be pursued.

Voting behavior, however, is not wholly dependent on the social, cultural, and psychological characteristics of voters.[12] The importance of variations in (1) local and national political structures, (2) election issues (programs, personalities, and party images), and (3) social and economic problems at different historical periods should be carefully considered both in planning and interpreting election studies. At this point, perhaps the greatest needs in voting research are continuing experimentation with social and psychological variables and also investigations of a wider variety of election types for fruitful comparisons and the inevitable checks on confident generalizations.

NOTES

CHAPTER 1

[1] Stuart Rice, *Quantitative Methods in Politics* (New York: Alfred A. Knopf, 1928).

[2] Austin Ranney, "The Utility and Limitations of Aggregate Data in the Study of Electoral Behavior," in Austin Ranney, ed., *Essays on the Behavioral Study of Politics* (Urbana: University of Illinois Press, 1962), p. 98.

[3] See especially V. O. Key, Jr., *Southern Politics in State and Nation* (New York: Alfred A. Knopf, 1949) and V. O. Key, Jr. and Frank Munger, "Social Determinism and Electoral Decision: The Case of Indiana," in Eugene Burdick and Arthur J. Brodbeck, eds., *American Voting Behavior* (Glencoe, Ill.: The Free Press, 1959), pp. 281-299.

[4] Paul F. Lazarsfeld, Bernard R. Berelson, and Hazel Gaudet, *The People's Choice*, 2d edition (New York: Columbia University Press, 1948).

[5] Bernard R. Berelson, Paul F. Lazarsfeld, and William N. McPhee, *Voting* (Chicago: University of Chicago Press, 1954).

[6] Scott Greer, *Governing the Metropolis* (New York: John Wiley and Sons, Inc., 1962), p. 96. See also Greer, "The Social Structure and Political Process of Suburbia," *American Sociological Review*, 25 (Aug., 1960), pp. 514-526.

[7] Angus Campbell, Gerald Gurin, and Warren E. Miller, *The Voter Decides* (New York: Harper, Row, and Co., 1954).

[8] Peter H. Rossi, "Four Landmarks in Voting Research," in Burdick and Brodbeck, *op. cit.*, p. 40.

[9] Key and Munger, "Social Determinism and Electoral Decision: The Case of Indiana," in Burdick and Brodbeck, *op. cit.*, p. 281.

[10] Angus Campbell, Philip Converse, Warren Miller, and Donald Stokes, *The American Voter* (New York: John Wiley and Sons, Inc., 1960), pp. 338-340.

[11] *Ibid.*, pp. 344-346.

[12] Philip Converse, "The Shifting Role of Class in Political Attitudes and Behavior," in Eleanor Maccoby, Theodore Newcomb, and Eugene Hartley, eds., *Readings in Social Psychology*, 3rd edition (New York: Holt, Rinehart and Winston, 1958), pp. 388-399.

[13] Campbell, Converse, Miller, and Stokes, *op. cit.*, p. 36.

[14] Charles H. Titus, "Voting in California Cities, 1900-1925," *Southwestern Political and Social Science Quarterly*, 8 (March, 1928), pp. 383-399; Roscoe C. Martin, "The Municipal Electorate: A Case Study," *Southwestern Social Science Quarterly*, 14 (December, 1933), pp. 193-237; Harold F. Gosnell, *Machine Politics: Chicago Model* (Chicago: University of Chicago Press, 1937); James K. Pollock, *Voting Behavior: A Case Study* (Ann Arbor: University of Michigan, Bureau of Government, 1939).

[15] Some suggestive comments on this topic are made in James S. Coleman, *Community Conflict* (Glencoe, Ill.: The Free Press, 1957), p. 19.

[16] R. D. McKenzie, "Community Forces: A Study of Non-Partisan Municipal Elections in Seattle," *Journal of Social Forces*, 2 (May, 1924), p. 564.

[17] Gosnell, *op. cit.*, p. 134.

[18] Leonard Reissman, K. H. Silvert, and Cliff W. Wing, Jr., *The New Orleans Voter: A Handbook of Political Description* (Tulane Studies in Political Science, vol. 2, 1955), p. 82. These data on low turnout do not agree with what little evidence there is on local attitudes toward local politics. For instance, Alfred DeGrazia found that only about 10 per cent of the citizenry claim to have less interest in local and state than in national politics. See DeGrazia, *The Western Public: 1952 and Beyond* (Stanford, Cal.: Stanford University Press, 1954), p. 172. In a New York mayoralty election, one-third of the population believed the results of the election would make no differ-

ence, but 43 per cent thought that it would. See Elmo Roper, "New York Elects O'Dwyer," *Public Opinion Quarterly*, 10 (Spring, 1946), pp. 53-56.

[19] William E. Wright, *Memphis Politics: A Study in Racial Bloc Voting*, Eagleton Institute Case Studies in Practical Politics, no. 27 (New York: The McGraw-Hill Co., Inc., 1962).

[20] Henry M. Alexander, *The Little Rock Recall Election*, Eagleton Institute Case Studies in Practical Politics, no. 17 (New York: The McGraw-Hill Co., Inc., 1960).

[21] Lawrence O'Rourke, *Voting Behavior in the Forty-Five Cities of Los Angeles County* (Los Angeles: University of California, Bureau of Governmental Research, 1953), p. 6. See also Ronald M. Ketchum, *Voting on Charter Amendments in Los Angeles* (Los Angeles, University of California, Bureau of Governmental Research, n.d.), p. 16.

[22] Greer, *Governing the Metropolis*, p. 90.

[23] *Ibid.*, pp. 91-93.

[24] Henry J. Schmandt, Paul G. Steinbicker, and George D. Wendel, *Metropolitan Reform in St. Louis* (New York: Holt, Rinehart and Winston, 1961).

[25] Fred Greenstein and Raymond E. Wolfinger, "The Suburbs and Shifting Party Loyalties," *Public Opinion Quarterly*, 22 (Winter, 1958-1959), pp. 473-482; James G. Manis and Leo C. Stine, "Suburban Residence and Political Behavior," *Public Opinion Quarterly*, 22 (Winter, 1958-1959), pp. 483-489; Edward C. Banfield, "The Politics of Metropolitan Area Organization," *Midwest Journal of Political Science*, 1 (May, 1957), pp. 77-91.

[26] V. O. Key, Jr., "Partisanship and the County Office: The Case of Ohio," *American Political Science Review*, 47 (June, 1953), pp. 525-532.

[27] Eugene C. Lee, *The Politics of Non-Partisanship* (Berkeley: University of California Press, 1960), pp. 59-60.

[28] Calvin F. Schmid, *Social Trends in Seattle* (Seattle: University of Washington Press, 1944), pp. 265-285.

[29] Oliver P. Williams and Charles R. Adrian, "The Insulation of Local Politics under the Nonpartisan Ballot," *American Political Science Review*, 53 (December, 1959), pp. 1052-1063.

[30] Charles R. Adrian, "A Typology for Non-Partisan Elections," *Western Political Quarterly*, 12 (June, 1959), pp. 449-458; Adrian, "Some General Characteristics of Non-Partisan Elections," *American Political Science Review*, 46 (September, 1952), pp. 766-776; George

W. Pearson, "Prediction in a Non-Partisan Election," *Public Opinion Quarterly*, 12 (Spring, 1948), pp. 112-117. Cf. Marvin Harder, *Non-Partisan Elections: A Political Illusion?* (New York: Henry Holt and Co., 1958).

[31] Edward C. Banfield, *Political Influence* (Glencoe, Ill.: The Free Press, 1961); J. Leiper Freeman, "Local Party Systems: Theoretical Considerations and a Case Analysis," *American Journal of Sociology*, 64 (November, 1958), pp. 282-289. See also Robert E. Agger and Daniel Goldrich, "Community Power Structure and Partisanship," *American Sociological Review*, 28 (August, 1958), pp. 383-391.

[32] Greer, *Governing the Metropolis*, pp. 102-128.

[33] Banfield, *Political Influence*, p. 248.

[34] Freeman, *op. cit.*, p. 282.

[35] James S. Bruner and Sheldon J. Korchin, "The Boss and the Vote: Case Study in City Politics," *Public Opinion Quarterly*, 10 (Spring, 1946), pp. 1-23.

[36] Robert A. Dahl, *Who Governs?* (New Haven: Yale University Press, 1961). Cf. Carl O. Smith and Stephen B. Sarasohn, "Hate Propaganda in Detroit," *Public Opinion Quarterly*, 10 (Spring, 1946), pp. 24-52.

[37] Walter C. Kaufman and Scott Greer, "Voting in a Metropolitan Community: An Application of Social Area Analysis," *Social Forces*, 38 (March, 1960), pp. 196-210; David A. Booth and Charles R. Adrian, "Elections and Community Power," *Journal of Politics*, 25 (February, 1963), pp. 107-118. See also J. D. Williams, *The Defeat of Home Rule in Salt Lake City*, Eagleton Institute Case Studies In Practical Politics, no. 2 (New York: The McGraw-Hill Co., Inc., 1960).

[38] Thomas A. F. Plaut, "Analysis of Voting Behavior on a Fluoridation Referendum," *Public Opinion Quarterly*, 23 (Summer, 1959-1960), pp. 213-222.

[39] Schmandt, Steinbicker, and Wendel, *op. cit.*

[40] Richard A. Watson and John H. Romani, "Metropolitan Government for Metropolitan Cleveland: An Analysis of the Voting Record," *Midwest Journal of Political Science*, 5 (November, 1961), pp. 365-390; James A. Norton, "Referenda Voting in a Metropolitan Area," *Western Political Quarterly*, 16 (March, 1963), pp. 195-214. Cf. Metropolitan Community Studies, Inc., *Metropolitan Challenge*, (Dayton, Ohio, November, 1959), p. 253.

CHAPTER 2

[1] League of Women Voters, *This Is DeKalb County* (1959), pp. 6-7.

[2] *Ibid.*, p. 56; DeKalb County Planning Department, *Population Report* (May, 1963), pp. 21-24; Atlanta Region Metropolitan Planning Commission, *Population-Housing As of April 1, 1960* (Atlanta, 1961), pp. 8-11.

[3] DeKalb County, *Bonds For Progress* (Decatur, 1961).

[4] *New York Times*, April 11, 1962; news release to radio and television stations, dated September 25, 1961.

[5] Data were obtained from the following invaluable source: Community Council of the Atlanta Area, *Atlanta's People: A Study of Selected Demographic Characteristics of the Population in the Atlanta Metropolitan Area, by Census Tracts, 1960* (Atlanta, 1963).

CHAPTER 3

[1] The following sources summarize and evaluate this mass of material in a very useful fashion, often with good bibliographies: Bernard Barber, *Social Stratification* (New York: Harcourt, Brace and World, 1957); Joseph A. Kahl, *The American Class Structure* (New York: Holt, Rinehart & Winston, 1957); W. Lloyd Warner *et al.*, *Social Class in America* (New York: Harper Torchbook, rev. ed., 1960); W. C. Bailey, *et al.*, *Bibliography on Status and Stratification* (New York: Social Science Research Council, 1952); Harold W. Pfautz, "The Current Literature on Social Stratification: Critique and Bibliography," *American Journal of Sociology*, 57 (January, 1953), pp. 391-418.

[2] See Barber, *op. cit.*, chapters 5-8; Kahl, *op. cit.*, chapters 3-6.

[3] Alvin Boskoff, Voting Patterns in the 1960 Presidential Election: An Application of a Voting Process Model to Atlanta (manuscript).

CHAPTER 4

[1] The concept of selective perception is well treated in Joseph T. Klapper, *The Effects of Mass Communication* (New York: The Free Press of Glencoe, 1960), pp. 21-23.

[2] Paul F. Lazarsfeld and Robert K. Merton, "Mass Communication, Popular Taste, and Organized Social Action," in Lyman Bryson, ed., *The Communication of Ideas* (New York: Harper, 1948), p. 113.

[3] Paul F. Lazarsfeld, Bernard Berelson, and Hazel Gaudet note, ". . . the more strongly partisan the person, the more likely he is to insulate himself from contrary points of view." See *The People's Choice* (New York: Columbia University Press, 1948), p. 89.

[4] Elihu Katz and Paul F. Lazarsfeld, *Personal Influence* (New York: The Free Press of Glencoe, 1955); Elihu Katz, "The Two-Step Flow of Communication," in Wilbur Schramm, ed., *Mass Communications* 2nd ed. (Urbana: University of Illinois Press, 1960), pp. 346-365; Wilbur Schramm and Richard F. Carter, "The Effectiveness of a Political Telethon," *Public Opinion Quarterly*, 23 (1959), pp. 121-126.

[5] Carl I. Hovland, "Effects of the Mass Media of Communication," in Gardner Lindzey, ed., *Handbook of Social Psychology* (Cambridge: Addison-Wesley, 1954), Vol. II, p. 1064.

[6] James S. Coleman, *Community Conflict* (New York: The Free Press of Glencoe, 1957), p. 4.

[7] Lazarsfeld, Berelson, and Gaudet, *op. cit.*, pp. 121-122.

[8] William Buchanan, "An Inquiry into Purposive Voting," *Journal of Politics*, 18 (1956), p. 293.

[9] Morris Janowitz, *The Community Press in an Urban Setting* (New York: The Free Press of Glencoe, 1952), pp. 132-141.

[10] "Bonds for Progress," p. 1.

[11] *Ibid.*

[12] Lazarsfeld, Berelson, and Gaudet, *op. cit.*, p. 102; Bernard Berelson, Paul F. Lazarsfeld, and William N. McPhee, *Voting* (Chicago: University of Chicago Press, 1954), p. 23. See also Kurt and Gladys E. Lang, "The Mass Media and Voting," in Eugene Burdick and Arthur Brodbeck, eds., *American Voting Behavior* (New York: The Free Press of Glencoe, 1959), pp. 217-235.

[13] The following are useful for understanding this topic: Herbert H. Hyman and Paul B. Sheatsley, "Some Reasons Why Information Campaigns Fail," *Public Opinion Quarterly*, 11 (1947), pp. 412-423; George Lundberg, "The Newspaper and Public Opinion," *Social Forces*, 4 (1926), pp. 709-715; G. W. Hartman, "A Field Experiment on the Comparative Effectiveness of 'Emotional' and 'Rational' Political Leaflets in Determining Election Results," *Journal of Abnormal and Social Psychology*, 31 (1936), pp. 99-114.

[14] Robert E. Lane, *Political Life* (New York: The Free Press of Glencoe, 1959), p. 89.

[15] Klapper, *op. cit.*, p. 99.

[16] Robert C. Wood, *Suburbia* (Boston: Houghton Mifflin, 1959), pp. 156-157.

[17] Coleman, *op. cit.*, p. 19. See also F. A. Plaut, "Analysis of Voting Behavior on a Fluoridation Referendum," *Public Opinion Quarterly*, 23, 1959), pp. 213-222, and R. L. Schank and Charles Goodman, "Reactions to Propaganda on Both Sides of a Controversial Issue," *Public Opinion Quarterly*, 3 (1939), pp. 107-112.

CHAPTER 5

[1] For a convenient summary of this research, see Robert E. Lane, *Political Life* (New York: The Free Press of Glencoe, 1959).

[2] Angus Campbell, Gerald Gurin, and Warren E. Miller, *The Voter Decides* (Evanston: Row, Peterson, 1954), p. 194. See also Angus Campbell, Philip E. Converse, Warren E. Miller, and Donald E. Stokes, *The American Voter* (New York: Wiley, 1960), pp. 105-106.

[3] Robert C. Wood, *Suburbia: Its People and Their Politics* (Boston: Houghton Mifflin, 1959), p. 156.

[4] Basil G. Zimmer and Amos Hawley, "Local Government as Viewed by Fringe Residents," *Rural Sociology*, 23 (1958), pp. 362-370.

[5] Scott Greer, *Governing the Metropolis* (New York: Wiley, 1962), p. 89.

[6] Scott Greer, "The Social Structure and Political Process of Suburbia," *American Sociological Review*, 25 (August, 1960), pp. 514-526.

[7] Robert K. Merton, *Social Theory and Social Structure* (New York: The Free Press of Glencoe, rev. ed. 1957), pp. 131-194.

[8] *Ibid.*, p. 185.

[9] Wendell Bell, "Anomie, Social Isolation, and the Class Structure," *Sociometry*, 20 (June, 1957), pp. 105-116. Ephraim H. Mizruchi, "Social Structure and Anomia in a Small City," *American Sociological Review*, 25 (October, 1960), pp. 645-654. See also Genevieve Knupfer, "Portrait of the Underdog," *Public Opinion Quarterly*, 11 (Spring, 1947), pp. 103-110.

[10] Leo Srole, "Social Integration and Certain Corollaries: An Exploratory Study," *American Sociological Review*, 21 (December, 1956), pp. 709-716.

[11] Murray B. Levin, *The Alienated Voter* (New York: Holt, Rinehart, and Winston, 1960); William Buchanan, "An Inquiry into Positive Voting," *Journal of Politics*, 18 (1956), pp. 281-296.

[12] James S. Coleman, *Community Conflict* (New York: The Free Press of Glencoe, 1957), p. 19.

CHAPTER 6

[1] These implications were brought to the attention of the authors by Professor William Buchanan. A study of the defeat of school bond elections has produced similar conclusions. The school bond elections, however, were held in an atmosphere of controversy quite unlike the situation in DeKalb County. Yet in both cases, the behavior of negative voters was similar. See John E. Horton and Wayne E. Thompson, "Powerlessness and Political Negativism: A Study of Defeated Local Referendums," *American Journal of Sociology*, 67 (March, 1962), pp. 485-493; Wayne E. Thompson and John E. Horton, "Political Alienation as a Force in Political Action," *Social Forces*, 38 (March, 1960), pp. 190-195.

[2] As a measure of socio-economic status an index was used that had been constructed from three variables: percentage of persons twenty-five years of age and over with eighth grade education or less; percentage of families with incomes of $5,000 or less in 1959; and percentage of males fourteen years of age or over employed in blue collar (unskilled) occupations. An average of these three measures was calculated for each census tract and subtracted from 100. This produced an index score in which the higher scores indicated higher socio-economic statuses of the tracts. Since votes are reported by *precinct*, which does not coincide with the census tract, it was necessary to transfer tract figures to precincts. This was done by superimposing a census tract map on a precinct map and estimating the degree of overlap, weighting each index according to the percentage of the precinct within a given tract. A composite index is a useful means of reducing the number of variables for analysis. See Eshref Shevky and Wendell

Bell, *Social Area Analysis* (Stanford, Calif.: Stanford University Press, 1959).

[3] Alvin Boskoff, *The Sociology of Urban Regions* (New York: Appleton-Century-Crofts, 1962), p. 133.

[4] Alvin Boskoff, "Differentiation of Life-Styles in a Residential Area: The Significance of Associational Types," (unpublished).

[5] Alvin Boskoff, "Suburban Residence and Changes in Voting Patterns," in Harmon Zeigler and M. Kent Jennings, eds., *The Electoral Process* (Englewood Cliffs, N. J.: Prentice-Hall, 1964).

[6] Scott Greer, "The Social Structure and Political Process of Suburbia," *American Sociological Review*, 25 (August, 1960), pp. 514-526.

[7] See Milton Friedman, *A Theory of the Consumption Function* (Princeton, N. J.: Princeton University Press, 1957), esp. pp. 206-208 and chap. 9; James S. Duesenberry, *Income, Saving and the Theory of Consumption Behavior* (Cambridge: Harvard University Press, 1949); Margaret G. Reid, *Housing and Income* (Chicago: University of Chicago Press, 1962).

[8] Scott Greer and Peter Orleans, "The Mass Society and the Parapolitical Structure," *American Sociological Review*, 27 (October, 1962), pp. 634-646.

[9] Karl Mannheim, *Ideology and Utopia* (New York: Harcourt, Brace, 1936), Chapters 3 and 5.

[10] David McClelland, *The Achieving Society* (Princeton, N. J.: D. Van Nostrand, 1961); David McClelland *et al.*, *Talent and Society* (Princeton, N. J.: D. Van Nostrand, 1958); David McClelland, *The Achievement Motive* (New York: Appleton-Century-Crofts, 1953).

[11] Daniel J. Boorstin, *The Genius of American Politics* (Chicago: University of Chicago Press, 1953).

[12] Austin Ranney, "The Utility and Limitation of Aggregate Data in the Study of Electoral Behavior," in Austin Ranney, ed., *Essays on the Behavioral Study of Politics* (Urbana: University of Illinois Press, 1962), p. 101; V. O. Key, "The Politically Relevant in Surveys," *Public Opinion Quarterly*, 24 (1960), pp. 54-61.

INDEX